Ace Your Data Science Interview
300 Questions And Answers
Machine Learning, Statistics, Databases and More

Zack Austin

Azure Publishing

Copyright 2017 by Azure Publishing. All rights reserved.

ISBN 978-1-387-43196-0

All rights reserved. This work may not be translated or copied in whole or in part without the written permission of the authors. No part of this publication may be reproduced, stored in a retrieval system, or transmitted in any form or by any means-electronic, mechanical, photocopying, scanning, or otherwise-without prior written permission of the authors, except as permitted under Section 107 or 108 of the 1976 United States Copyright Act.

Limit of Liability/Disclaimer of Warranty: While the authors have used their best efforts in preparing this book, they make no representation or warranties with respect to the accuracy or completeness of the contents of this book and specifically disclaim any implied warranties of merchantability or fitness for a particular purpose. No warranty may be created or extended by sales representatives or written sales materials. The advice and strategies contained herein may not be suitable for your situation. You should consult with a professional where appropriate. The authors shall not be liable for any loss of profit or any other commercial damages, including but not limited to special, incidental, consequential, or other damages.

The use in this publication of tradenames, trademarks, service marks, and similar terms, even if they are not identified as such, is not to be taken as an expression of opinion as to whether or not they are subject to proprietary rights.

All product names, logos, and brands are property of their respective owners. All company, product and service names used in this book are for identification purposes only. Use of these names, logos, and brands does not imply endorsement. Azure Publishing is not associated with any product or vendor mentioned in this publication.

CONTENT EDITORS: BHAVANI BHARADWAJ, BAISHALI MANDAL

Contents

1	Statistics	9
2	Linear Models and Regression	19
3	Relational Algebra	29
4	SQL	31
5	NoSQL	41
6	Hadoop	51
7	Machine Learning	55
8	Bioinformatics	75
9	Python and Libraries	79
10	Answers To Statistics	83
11	Answers To Linear Models and Regression	87
12	Answers To Relational Algebra	91
13	Answers To SQL	93
14	Answers To NoSQL	99
15	Answers To Hadoop	103

16 Answers To Machine Learning	105
17 Answers To Bioinformatics	115
18 Answers To Python and Libraries	117

About The Author

Zack Austin has been building large scale enterprise systems for clients in media, telecom, financial services and publishing since 2001. His current focus is using machine learning to analyze customer behavior in online and offline retail. He is based in New York City.

Outline

Chapter 1 covers foundations of statistics required for any small or large scale data science project.

Chapter 2 tests you on the most common data science techniques, linear models and regression.

Chapter 3 covers the building blocks of most databases, relational algebra.

Chapter 4 deals with SQL (structured query language), the workhorse of all data intensive applications.

Chapter 5 covers NoSQL, the set of technologies that offer alternatives to relational databases.

Chapter 6 tests your expertise on Hadoop, one of the current leading standards for dealing with big data.

Chapter 7 covers several topics in the area of machine learning.

Chapter 8 focuses on techniques and tools used in the field of bioinformatics.

Chapter 9 covers the programming language Python, and various Python libraries used for data and analytics.

Statistics

1. The temperature in degrees Celsius over 4 days in Oslo city in October was 12, 15, 14, and 9. What is the mean temperature?

   A. 13
   B. 14
   C. 12.5
   D. 14.5

2. What is Multivariate Analysis?

   A. Type of statistical analysis than can study basic sets of data like software, etc. by analyzing dual outcome variables at a time.
   B. Type of statistical analysis than can study complex sets of data like software, etc. by analyzing more than one outcome variable at a time.
   C. Type of statistical analysis that involves the study of 2 variables and determines the unique factual relationship between them.
   D. The simplest type of statistical analysis that describes patterns in data by analyzing only one outcome variable for every observation.

3. What is a Bar Graph?

   A. Graph used to display trends in data over a time period (x-axis), where data is denoted as a series of points or markers joined by straight lines (y-axis).
   B. Graph that breaks down categorical data into groups, and represents each group as a slice, whose angle and area correspond to its numerical proportion.
   C. Graph that breaks down categorical data into groups, and shows them as rectangular bars, whose lengths and heights are proportional to the values they represent.
   D. Graph that breaks down categorical data into groups, and shows them as a series of dots representing continuous data.

4. What is the type of statistical analysis that involves the study of two variables and determines the factual relationship between them, called?

    A. Multivariate Analysis.
    B. Univariate Analysis.
    C. Bivariate Analysis.
    D. Covariate Analysis.

5. What is a Paired t-test?

    A. Similar to the t-test, only, the samples have matched pairs of similar units, or a group of units which is tested twice.
    B. A statistical test where the sampling distribution of the test statistic is used for analyzing categorical data.
    C. A comparison procedure where the family-wise error rate is divided by the number of comparisons.
    D. Analysis of two population means where the test statistic follows a t-distribution under the null hypothesis.

6. What is the Empirical Rule?

    A. Rule used to remember the percentage (65.27
    B. Rule that derives a regression equation by adding or subtracting one variable at a time from the regression equation.
    C. Rule used to remember the percentage (68.27
    D. The rule that gives the probability of the joint occurrence of events that are independent.

7. What is a Boxplot?

    A. One-dimensional graph that depicts groups of numerical data through their quartiles, based on the five-number summary.
    B. One-dimensional graph that breaks down categorical data into groups, and represents each group as a slice, whose angle and area correspond to its numerical proportion.
    C. One-dimensional graph used to display trends in data over a time period (x-axis), where data is denoted as a series of points or markers joined by straight lines (y-axis).
    D. One-dimensional graph that breaks down categorical data into groups, and shows them as a rectangular bar.

8. What is Test Statistic?

    A. Data that systematically undermeasure, or overmeasure the true result of a study, due to various reasons such as a faulty design of the study, leading questions, etc.
    B. Statistic that represents the distance between the actual sample results and the claimed population value, in terms of number of standard errors.
    C. Hypothesis related to the form of probability distribution for a specified population, or the probabilistic

10

technique that should deliver the observations.

D. The probability of finding the more extreme, or observed results for a statistical model, when the null hypothesis is true for the study question.

9. Which of the following best describes a Pie Chart?

   A. Circular chart that breaks down categorical data into groups, and shows them as rectangular bars, whose lengths and heights are proportional to the values they represent.

   B. Circular chart that breaks down categorical data into groups, and shows them as a series of dots representing continuous data.

   C. Circular chart that breaks down categorical data into groups, and represents each group as a slice, whose angle and area correspond to its numerical proportion.

   D. Circular chart used to display trends in data over a time period (x-axis), where data is denoted as a series of points or markers joined by straight lines (y-axis).

10. When the default hypothesis states that the population parameter is equal to the claimed value, and is assumed to be true until proven otherwise, what is it called?

    A. Logical Hypothesis.

    B. Alternative Hypothesis (Ha).

    C. Empirical Hypothesis.

    D. Null Hypothesis (H0).

11. What is Combination?

    A. Total number of ways in which a particular number of objects, taken from a bigger group of objects, can be ordered.

    B. Occurs when in a multiple regression model, one predictor variable can be linearly predicted from others with significant accuracy.

    C. Total number of ways in which objects can be chosen from a pool, without giving any importance to the order in which they are organized.

    D. Value that measures the proportion of positives which are accurately identified as such. E.g. percentage of sick people, correctly identified as having the condition.

12. What is a Histogram?

    A. A type of bar chart which accurately represents the probability distribution of a quantitative variable in graphical manner.

    B. A type of chart used to display trends in data over a time period (x-axis), where data is denoted as a series of points or markers joined by straight lines (y-axis).

    C. Circular chart that breaks down categorical data into

groups, and represents each group as a slice, whose angle and area correspond to its numerical proportion.

D. One-dimensional graph that depicts groups of numerical data through their quartiles, based on the five-number summary.

13. Which of the following best describes p-value?

    A. The probability that separates the higher half of a data set, a probability distribution, or a population, from its lower half.

    B. The probability that is used to determine the central tendency of a data set, a probability distribution, or a population.

    C. The probability of finding the more extreme, or observed results for a statistical model, when the null hypothesis is true for the study question.

    D. Hypothesis related to the form of probability distribution for a specified population, or the probabilistic technique that should deliver the observations.

14. Which of the following best describes Multicollinearity?

    A. Multicollinearity occurs when a set of vectors are said to be linearly dependent, and one of the vectors in the set are a linear combination of the others.

    B. Multicollinearity occurs when the total number of ways in which a particular number of objects, taken from a bigger group of objects, can be ordered.

    C. Multicollinearity occurs when in a multiple regression model, one predictor variable can be linearly predicted from others with significant accuracy.

    D. Multicollinearity occurs when the total number of ways in which objects can be chosen from a pool, without giving any importance to the order in which they are organized.

15. Which of the following is a step in calculating Confidence Interval?

    A. Determine the Margin of Error.

    B. Find the Null Hypothesis for this statistic.

    C. Find central limits.

    D. Choose the population statistic.

16. You want to obtain a measure of variation that is based on the five-number summary by finding the interquartile range. What is the interquartile range formula?

    A. IQR = Q1 - Q4. Which means, Interquartile Range is the 1st quartile subtracted from the 4th quartile.

    B. IQR = Q3 - Q1. Which means, Interquartile Range

12

is the 1st quartile subtracted from the 3rd quartile.
C. IQR = Q1 - Q3. Which means, Interquartile Range is the 3rd quartile subtracted from the 1st quartile.
D. IQR = Q3 - Q2. Which means, Interquartile Range is the 1st quartile subtracted from the 2nd quartile.

17. Which of the following best describes Power Analysis?

    A. Applied in calculating the t-distribution, likely to be found in a study with a given sample.
    B. Applied in calculating the sum of squares of subject totals, to remove the effects from the error term.
    C. Used to calculate from a sample and is used primarily to describe the sample.
    D. Used to calculate the minimum sample size required to be fairly likely to find an effect of a given size.

18. Which of the following can be best described as Univariate Analysis?

    A. Type of statistical analysis than can study complex sets of data like software, etc. by analyzing more than one outcome variable at a time.
    B. The simplest type of statistical analysis that describes patterns in data by analyzing only one outcome variable for every observation.
    C. The simplest type of statistical analysis that describes functions in data by analyzing only one outcome variable for multiple observations.
    D. Type of statistical analysis that involves the study of 2 variables and determines the unique factual relationship between them.

19. Which of the following is a relevant sample percentile in the context of the five-number summary?

    A. The sample minimum, which is the mean observation.
    B. The 50th percentile or the mean.
    C. The third quartile, or the 75th percentile.
    D. The sample maximum or the 75th percentile.

20. The temperature in degrees Celsius over 4 days in Prague city in October was 12, 15, 14, and 9. What is the median?

    A. 13
    B. 14
    C. 14.5
    D. 12.5

21. Which of the following best describes Standard Deviation?

    A. Type of statistical analysis that involves the study of 2 variables and determines the factual relationship between them.

13

B. The statistic that reports the relative standing of the mean, median, and SD, indicating the value below which, a given percentage of observations fall.

C. A measure of statistical dispersion that shows the distance taken up by the innermost 50

D. The statistic that divides an ordered distribution into four parts, which are the quarters of the population.

22. You find that a null hypothesis that is not true, and is not rejected. What is the type of error?

A. Type 2 Error.

B. Type 3 Error.

C. Type 0 Error.

D. Type 1 Error.

23. Which of the following best describes Standard Deviation?

A. Standard Deviation (SD) is the value that denotes the variation in numerical data by measuring the concentration of the data around the mean.

B. Standard Deviation (SD) is the value that separates the higher half of a data set, a probability distribution, or a population, from its lower half.

C. Standard Deviation (SD) is the average used to determine the central tendency of a data set, a probability distribution, or a population.

D. Standard Deviation (SD) is the simplest type of statistical analysis that describes patterns in data by analyzing only one outcome variable for every observation.

24. Which of the following best describes Stacking?

A. An ensemble learning meta-algorithm that uses intuitive justification and an iterative model to reduce bias and variance in supervised learning.

B. Meta-algorithm that improves the accuracy and stability of machine learning algorithms by combining predictions through methods of averaging or voting.

C. Method of using many diverse models in order to compute the initial prediction and mixing predictions to achieve a better final prediction.

D. Method of training an algorithm to combine the predictions of multiple models or algorithms as additional inputs to the already available data.

25. Which of the following is a common measure of relative standing?

A. Quartiles.

B. Deciles.

C. Fractiles.

D. Quantiles.

26. What is Permutation?

A. Total number of ways in which objects can be chosen from a pool, without giving any importance to the order in which they are organized.

B. Total number of ways in which a particular number of objects, taken from a bigger group of objects, can be ordered.

C. Occurs when in a multiple regression model, one predictor variable can be linearly predicted from others with significant accuracy.

D. Value that measures the proportion of positives which are accurately identified as such. E.g. percentage of sick people, correctly identified as having the condition.

27. In the context of a five-number summary, which of the following is a valid sample percentile?

   A. The sample minimum, which is the mean observation.
   B. The sample maximum or the 75th percentile.
   C. The 50th percentile or the mean.
   D. The first quartile, or the 25th percentile of the sample.

28. Which of the following best describes power analysis?

   A. Applied in calculating the sum of squares of subject totals, to remove the effects from the error term.
   B. Applied in calculating the t-distribution, likely to be found in a study with a given sample.
   C. Used to calculate from a sample and is used primarily to describe the sample.
   D. Applied in calculating the minimum effect size, likely to be found in a study with a given sample.

29. Which of the following best describes Margin of Error (MOE)?

   A. The measure of the sample statistic that occurs when a null hypothesis is not true and is not rejected.
   B. The measure of how close the sample statistic is expected to be, to the population parameter being observed.
   C. The measure of interval estimate computed from the observed data of a population parameter.
   D. The measure of the sample statistic that occurs when a null hypothesis is true and is rejected.

30. The difference in value for every variable in a given data set, is called as:

   A. Standard Deviation.
   B. Percentile.
   C. Mean.
   D. Variation.

31. A hypothesis test has one statement that the mean completion time for a survey is 45 minutes,

15

and another statement that the time is > 45 minutes. The second statement is called as:

A. Alternative Hypothesis (Ha).
B. Null Hypothesis (H0).
C. Logical Hypothesis.
D. Empirical Hypothesis.

32. When a null hypothesis that is true, is rejected, what is the error called?

A. Type 2 Error.
B. Type 1 Error.
C. Type 0 Error.
D. Type 3 Error.

33. The data that represents characteristics of the observed in numerical values, is called as:

A. Count Data.
B. Exploratory Data.
C. Frequency Data.
D. Categorical Data.

34. What is the standard deviation of a statistic's (usually the mean) sampling distribution, or in some cases, an estimate of such a standard deviation, called?

A. df error.
B. Standard Error (SE).
C. Error rate per comparison (PC).
D. Margin of Error (MOE).

35. A type of chart that is used to display trends in data over a time period (x-axis) where data is denoted as a series of points or markers joined by straight lines (y-axis) is called as:

A. Boxplot.
B. Time Chart/Line Graph.
C. Bar Graph.
D. Box-and-whisker plot.

36. What is the concept called, for the statistic that divides an ordered distribution into four parts, which are the quarters of the population?

A. Quartiles.
B. Quintiles.
C. Quantiles.
D. Deciles.

37. When a value measures the proportion of positives which are accurately identified, e.g. percentage of sick people correctly identified as having the condition, what is it called?

A. Combination.
B. Sensitivity.
C. Multicollinearity.
D. Permutation.

38. What is the concept called, for a type of interval estimate computed from the observed data of a population parameter?

A. Critical Interval.
B. Interval Scale.
C. Confidence Interval.
D. Interval Estimate.

39. Analysis of two population means where the test statistic follows a t-distribution under the null hypothesis, is called as:

A. t-test.
B. Bonferroni test.

C. Paired t-test.

D. Chi-square test.

40. In the context of the five-number summary, which of the following is a relevant sample percentile?

    A. The second quartile, or the 25th percentile of the sample.
    B. The sample minimum, which is the smallest observation.
    C. The sample maximum or the 75th percentile.
    D. The 50th percentile, or the mean.

41. What is Interquartile Range?

    A. The range between two hinges and derived by subtracting Q1 from Q3.
    B. The range over which X or Y varies is artificially limited, and derived by subtracting Q1 from Q2.
    C. A measure of statistical function that shows the distance taken up by the independent 50% of the data, derived at, by subtracting Q1 from Q2.
    D. A measure of statistical dispersion that shows the distance taken up by the innermost 50% of the data, derived at, by subtracting Q1 from Q3.

42. You are exploring a probabilistic technique that offers a mechanism to make quantitative decisions and has enough evidence to reject or accept a conjecture. What is the technique called?

    A. Descriptive Data Analysis.
    B. Statistical Hypothesis.
    C. P-Value Testing.
    D. Exploratory Data Analysis.

2

Linear Models and Regression

1. How is a Continuous Random Variable defined?

   A. Random variables that usually represent counts, and whose possible outcomes can be listed using whole numbers.

   B. Random variables that usually represent measurements, and whose possible outcomes can be described only using an interval of real numbers.

   C. Random variables that have ordinal intervals or ratio scales and are measured on a numeric scale for meaningful arithmetic operations.

   D. Random variables that changes randomly as per a pattern, and whose possible values are numerical outcomes of a random occurrence.

2. When a model cannot capture the underlying trend in the data, resulting in inadequate predictive performance, what is the concept called?

   A. Overfitting.
   B. Regularization.
   C. Underfitting.
   D. Normalization.

3. Which of the following can be considered as a condition for a Binomial Distribution?

   A. Are the trials flexible?
   B. Is the number of trials fixed?
   C. Does the variance provide the spread?
   D. Does each trial have multiple outcomes?

4. You are looking at a regression technique that is used primarily for numeric prediction, that expresses the class as a linear combination of the attributes. What is the technique called?

   A. Linear Regression.
   B. Logistic Regression.
   C. Multiple Regression.
   D. Multinomial Regression.

5. You want to know more about the Generalized Linear Model (GLM). Which of the following best describes GLM?

   A. A generalization of linear regression where significant reduction in the complexity of the related statistical theory is attainable.

   B. A generalization of linear regression technique used primarily for numeric prediction that expresses the class as a linear combination of the attributes.

   C. A generalization of linear regression technique creates a linear model based on a transformed target variable, where the dependent variable is categorical.

   D. A generalization of linear regression that is flexible, and allows for response variables that have other kind of error distribution models than a normal distribution.

6. What is a Linear model?

   A. A type of regression model where significant reduction in the complexity of the related statistical theory is attainable.

   B. A type of regression model where a two-parameter family of continuous probability distributions, alpha and theta being the two free parameters.

   C. A type of regression model which is used to predict the value of a variable based on the value of two or more other variables.

   D. A type of regression model where all the probabilities of all possible values of a discrete random variable, occurring in an experiment. Denoted as p(x).

7. Which of the following best describes the General Linear Model?

   A. Written as X=YB-U, this is a statistical linear model.

   B. Written as Y=XB+U, this is a statistical linear model.

   C. Written as X=YB+U, this is a statistical linear model.

   D. Written as U=XB-Y, this is a statistical linear model.

8. Which of the following best describes the traveling salesman problem?

   A. A deterministic polynomial-time-hard problem in combinatorial explosion, significant in the fields of theoretical computer science and management research.

   B. A non-deterministic quasi-homogeneous-time-hard problem in combinatorial optimization, significant in the fields of abstract algebra and operations research.

   C. A deterministic trinomial-time-hard problem in combinatorial methods, significant in the fields of algebraic geometry and management research.

D. A nondeterministic polynomial-time-hard problem in combinatorial optimization, significant in the fields of theoretical computer science and operations research.

9. What is the method of adding more data as a countermeasure against overfitting, or to tackle an ill-posed problem, called?

    A. Underfitting.
    B. Regularization.
    C. Overfitting.
    D. Normalization.

10. What is Matrix transpose?

    A. The inverse of a matrix (table) showing the pairwise correlations between all variables.
    B. Operator that creates another matrix by switching the row and column indices of the matrix, which means flipping the matrix over its diagonal.
    C. Operator that creates a matrix of coded or dummy variables representing group membership.
    D. The inverse of a square matrix, which, in case the invertible matrix is A, is denoted as A to the power minus one.

11. What is the random variable that usually represent counts, and whose possible outcomes can be listed using whole numbers, called?

    A. Qualitative Random Variable.
    B. Continuous Random Variable.
    C. Categorical Random Variable.
    D. Discrete Random Variable.

12. What is Gamma Distribution?

    A. A type of general distribution which is a two-parameter family of continuous probability distributions, alpha and theta being the two free parameters.
    B. Continuous probability distribution of a random variable with a normally distributed logarithm.
    C. The discrete probability distribution of the number of successes in a sequence of 'n' independent experiments, each asking a yes-no question.
    D. A discrete probability distribution that is valid only if the events happen independently of the time since the last event, and with a known constant.

13. Which of the following best describes t-distribution?

    A. A family of distributions identical to the normal distribution, but used when the sample size is much smaller, and the population SD is unknown.
    B. The discrete probability distribution of the number of successes in a sequence of 'n' independent experiments, each asking a yes-no question.

C. Most commonly used normal distribution where the mean is zero, and the SD is 1. It is used to find percentiles and probabilities for regular normal distributions.

D. A type of general distribution which is a two-parameter family of continuous probability distributions, alpha and theta being the two free parameters.

14. What is Normality Assumption?

A. Normality assumptions can be tested as a hypothesis based on parameter estimation.

B. Normality assumptions can be tested as a null hypothesis, using the Shapiro-Wilk test.

C. Normality assumptions can be tested as a hypothesis, using the Tukey's test.

D. Normality assumptions can be tested as a hypothesis, using the Breusch and Pagan test.

15. You want to know more about the conditions for a Binomial Distribution. Which of the following is a valid condition?

A. Are the trials independent?

B. Does the variance provide the spread?

C. Is the number of trials dynamic?

D. Does each trial have multiple outcomes?

16. The inverse of a square matrix, which, in case the invertible matrix is A, is denoted as A to the power minus one, is called as:

A. Matrix transpose.
B. Covariance matrix.
C. Matrix inverse.
D. Design matrix.

17. Which of the following best describes Poisson Distribution?

A. The discrete probability distribution of the number of successes in a sequence of 'n' independent experiments, each asking a yes-no question.

B. A type of general distribution which is a two-parameter family of continuous probability distributions, alpha and theta being the two free parameters.

C. A discrete probability distribution that is valid only if the events happen independently of the time since the last event, and with a known constant.

D. Continuous probability distribution of a random variable with a normally distributed logarithm.

18. Which of the following is a relevant parameter that defines Normal Distribution?

A. The variance, which refers to the center of the curve.

B. The Mu, which provides the spread.

C. The Standard Deviation (SD), which refers to the center of the curve.

D. The Mu, which refers to the center of the curve.

19. What is a Random Variable?

   A. A variable, measurement, or characteristic that has ordinal intervals or ratio scales and are measured on a numeric scale for meaningful arithmetic operations.

   B. A variable, measurement, or characteristic that changes randomly as per a pattern, and whose possible values are numerical outcomes of a random occurrence.

   C. A variable that summarizes the relationship of small number of values and a table of frequencies classified according to the values of the variables in question.

   D. A variable, measurement, or characteristic that are categorical and are not numerical, and is the key to understanding statistics.

20. What is the distribution for continuous data called, in a symmetrical bell curve, with the center of the curve representing the highest probability density?

   A. Probability Distribution.
   B. Lognormal Distribution.
   C. Poisson Distribution.
   D. Normal Distribution.

21. You are looking at a regression technique that creates a linear model based on a transformed target variable where the dependent variable is categorical. What is the concept called?

   A. Logistic Regression.
   B. Multinomial Regression.
   C. Multiple Regression.
   D. Linear Regression.

22. What is the continuous probability distribution of a random variable with a normally distributed logarithm, called?

   A. Normal Distribution.
   B. Poisson Distribution.
   C. Lognormal Distribution.
   D. Logistic Distribution.

23. You want to know more about the Probability Density of the Bell Curve in a Normal Distribution. Which of the following is the most relevant in the context?

   A. The standard deviation is at the center, and has the highest probability density, and so, as you move away from this center, the density increases.

   B. Both the mean and the median are at the extreme ends of the bell curve and have the highest probability density, and so, as you move away from this center, the density decreases.

   C. Both the mean and the median are at the center, and have the highest probability density, and so, as you move away from this center, the density decreases.

23

D. The standard deviation is at the center, and has the lowest probability density, and so, as you move away from this center, the density increases.

24. What is Overfitting?

    A. Occurs when a model cannot capture the underlying trend in the data, resulting in inadequate predictive performance.

    B. Occurs when the performance of a model on new data is positively affected because of the basic nature of the model, and picking up even the noise in the training data.

    C. Occurs when the performance of a model on new data is negatively affected because of the model being too complex, and picking up even the noise in the training data.

    D. Method of adding more data as a countermeasure against overfitting, or to tackle an ill-posed problem.

25. Which of the following best describes Probability Distribution?

    A. Normally expected distribution for continuous data, in a symmetrical bell curve, with the center of the curve representing the highest probability density.

    B. A function showing all the probabilities of all possible values of a discrete random variable, occurring in an experiment.

    C. A function showing the probability distribution of a random variable with a normally distributed logarithm.

    D. A function showing all the probabilities of a given number of events happening in a fixed interval of time and/or space.

26. You want to know about a type of variance analysis that is used to check if there are statistically significant differences between 3 or more population means. What is the concept called?

    A. One-way Analysis of Variance.

    B. Multivariate analysis of variance (MANOVA).

    C. Two-way Analysis of Variance.

    D. Residual Variance.

27. Which of the following best describes Homoscedasticity assumption?

    A. Homoscedasticity assumptions can be tested as a hypothesis, using the Breusch and Pagan test.

    B. Homoscedasticity assumptions can be tested as a hypothesis, using the Tukey's test.

    C. Homoscedasticity assumptions can be tested as a null hypothesis, using the Shapiro-Wilk test.

24

D. Homoscedasticity assumptions can be tested as a hypothesis based on parameter estimation.

28. What is Binomial Distribution?

    A. The discrete probability distribution of the number of successes in a sequence of 'n' independent experiments, each asking a yes-no question.

    B. A discrete probability distribution that is valid only if the events happen independently of the time since the last event, and with a known constant.

    C. Continuous probability distribution of a random variable with a normally distributed logarithm.

    D. A type of general distribution which is a two-parameter family of continuous probability distributions, alpha and theta being the two free parameters.

29. You are looking for a statistical technique that is used to find percentiles for regular normal distributions having a mean of zero and a SD of 1. What is the technique called?

    A. Rademacher distribution.

    B. t-distribution.

    C. Skellam distribution.

    D. z-distribution.

30. You want to know more about Bernoulli Distribution. Which of the following best describes the concept?

    A. A discrete binomial distribution where a single trial is conducted, which has two possible outcomes, success (n=1), and failure (n=0).

    B. The discrete probability distribution of the number of successes in a sequence of 'n' independent experiments, each asking a yes-no question.

    C. A type of general distribution which is a two-parameter family of continuous probability distributions, alpha and theta being the two free parameters.

    D. A discrete probability distribution that is valid only if the events happen independently of the time since the last event, and with a known constant.

31. You want to know more about Robust Test. Which of the following best describes the concept?

    A. Alternative assumption testing method used when linearity or normascedasticity assumptions produce results with unequal variances.

    B. Alternative assumption testing method used when normality or distributional assumptions produce results with unequal variances.

    C. Alternative assumption testing method used when normality or homoscedasticity assumptions produce results with unequal variances.

D. Alternative assumption testing method used when normality or heteroscedasticity assumptions produce results with unequal variances.

32. What is Sampling Distribution?

A. Most commonly used normal distribution where the mean is zero, and the SD is 1. It is used to find percentiles and probabilities for regular normal distributions.

B. Probability distribution of a given statistic, based on a random sample that hugely simplify the ways to reach statistical inference.

C. The discrete probability distribution of the number of successes in a sequence of 'n' independent experiments, each asking a yes-no question.

D. A family of distributions identical to the normal distribution, but used when the sample size is much smaller, and the population SD is unknown.

33. What is the standard deviation of a statistic's (usually the mean) sampling distribution, or in some cases, an estimate of such a standard deviation, called?

A. df error.

B. Standard Error (SE).

C. Error rate per comparison (PC).

D. Margin of Error (MOE).

34. What is a Two-way Analysis of Variance?

A. Type of variance analysis used to check if there are statistically significant differences between 3 or more population means.

B. Type of variance analysis used to check the differences of variance with two or more dependent variables.

C. Type of variance analysis used to compare the differences in mean between groups that are split on two factors or independent variables.

D. Type of variance analysis used to check the square of the standard error of estimate.

35. What is the statistical process that determines the strength of the relationship between one fixed dependent variable, and a series of changing independent variables called?

A. Linear Model.

B. Normal Distribution.

C. Regression.

D. Gamma Distribution.

36. Which of the following can be best described as the General Linear Model?

A. X=YB-U, where: Y is a matrix with series of multivariate measurements; X is a design matrix; B is a matrix of parameters to be estimated; and U is a matrix of noise.

B. U=YB+X, where: Y is a matrix with series of multivariate measurements; X is a design matrix; B is a matrix of parameters to be estimated; and U is a matrix of noise.

C. Y=XB+U, where: Y is a matrix with series of multivariate measurements; X is a design matrix; B is a matrix of parameters to be estimated; and U is a matrix of noise.

D. X=UB-Y, where: Y is a matrix with series of multivariate measurements; X is a design matrix; B is a matrix of parameters to be estimated; and U is a matrix of noise.

37. When a discrete probability distribution asserts the probability of a given number of events happening in a fixed interval of time and/or space, what is the distribution called?

A. Normal Distribution.

B. Logistic Distribution.

C. Poisson Distribution.

D. Lognormal Distribution.

3

Relational Algebra

1. Which of the following can be best described as the Rename operation in Relational Algebra?

   A. Operation that can combine information from two relations.
   B. Operation that can yield results that include the phrase "for all".
   C. A binary operation that can create an implicit join clause based on common columns in the two tables that are being joined.
   D. A unary operation that lets you assign a name to the results of a relational-algebra expression.

2. What is the binary operation that can create an implicit join clause based on common columns in the two tables that are being joined, called?

   A. Natural Join.
   B. Cartesian Product.
   C. Division.
   D. Assignment.

3. What is a family of algebras used for defining queries on relational databases, and modeling the data stored in them, giving a theoretical foundation, called?

   A. Relational Algebra.
   B. Quaternion algebra.
   C. Relation algebra.
   D. Birman-Wenzl algebra

4. What is the Union operation in Relational Algebra?

   A. A binary operation that returns the results that appear in one or both of the two relations.
   B. Operation that yields tuples that are present in one relation and not in another.
   C. A unary operation that returns its argument relation with a few attributes excluded.
   D. A unary operation that selects tuples that satisfy a specific predicate.

5. Which of the following can be considered as Fundamental operations in Relational Algebra?

    A. Intersect.
    B. Set Union.
    C. Select.
    D. Insert.

6. What is an operation that assigns expressions to a temporary relation variable?

    A. Cartesian Product.
    B. Natural Join.
    C. Division.
    D. Assignment.

7. What is the Select operation in Relational Algebra?

    A. Operation that yields tuples that are present in one relation and not in another.
    B. A unary operation that returns its argument relation with a few attributes excluded.
    C. A binary operation that returns the results that appear in one or both of the two relations.
    D. A unary operation that selects tuples that satisfy a specific predicate.

8. You want to know more about a unary operation that returns its argument relation with a few attributes excluded. What is the operation called?

    A. Set Difference.
    B. Union.
    C. Project.
    D. Select.

9. Which of the following best describes Set-intersection?

    A. Operation that yields tuples that are present in one relation and not in another.
    B. Operation that can combine information from two relations.
    C. Operation that yields the tuples that are present in both relations the operation is applying to.
    D. Operation that can yield results that include the phrase "for all".

10. What is the operation that yields tuples that are present in one relation and not in another, called?

    A. Set difference.
    B. Select.
    C. Project.
    D. Union.

11. You want to know more about an operation that can combine information from two relations. What is the operation called?

    A. Natural Join.
    B. Division.
    C. Assignment.
    D. Cartesian Product.

12. What is the Division operation in Relational Algebra?

    A. Cartesian Product.
    B. Division.
    C. Natural Join.
    D. Assignment.

4

SQL

1. Which of the following best describes the Update Row command??

    A. Statement used to change a row in an existing table in a database. However, all records will be changed if the 'WHERE' clause is not used.

    B. Statement used to change the data in a row of a table. You can choose to update all the rows at once, or, choose a subset with the use of a condition.

    C. Statement used to modify a table definition, and all corresponding details including all the data, permission specifications, constraints, triggers, and indexes.

    D. Statement used to modify a new row to an existing table in a database.

2. What is the Time data type?

    A. A data type that can store a point in time, including hours, minutes, seconds and usually, milliseconds.

    B. A sequence of characters that can either be any kind of variable, or a literal constant.

    C. Set of binary data stored in a database management system as a single entity, primarily in the form of multimedia objects like audio, images, etc.

    D. A data type that can store a date and time value.

3. What are ACID properties?

    A. Properties of binary data stored in a database management system as a single entity, primarily in the form of multimedia objects like audio, images, etc.

    B. Properties of synchronizing databases with each other based on specific criteria set by the programmer, in order to securely backup data and avoid data loss.

    C. Mechanisms in RDBMS that protect the integrity of

data during server failures or when multiple users try to access the same data at the same time.

D. Properties of database transactions that aim at guaranteeing validity despite events of power failures, errors, etc.

4. Which of the following best describes Relational Algebra?

   A. A family of algebras used primarily to manage data in a relational database management system, which uses a single command to access many records.

   B. A family of algebras used in open-source relational framework based on Java that is ideal for distributed storage and handling of very large amounts of data.

   C. A family of algebras used for defining queries on relational databases, and modeling the data stored in them, giving a theoretical foundation.

   D. A family of algebras used in largely distributed database environment that allows for high-speed, ad-hoc analysis and organizing of high-volume data types.

5. What are Ordered Indices?

   A. Simplest way of optimizing an SQL database, where the contents of the database are organized in the same way as data is requested frequently.

   B. Operation that returns all the records from the table on the right, and only the matched records from the table on the left.

   C. Operation where the resulting table retains all the rows even if there are no matching rows.

   D. A type of lookup table that can be created for each column that is important, in order to optimize the performance of SQL databases.

6. Which of the following best describes Replication?

   A. Process of synchronizing databases with each other based on specific criteria set by the programmer, in order to securely backup data and avoid data loss.

   B. Simplest way of optimizing an SQL database, where the contents of the database are organized in the same way as data is requested frequently.

   C. A type of lookup table that can be created for each column that is important, in order to optimize the performance of SQL databases.

   D. Operation that returns all the records from the table on the right, and only the matched records from the table on the left.

7. When a stored procedure executes commonly required actions automatically during a specific event occurring in the database server, what is this called?

A. Stored Procedure.

B. Index.

C. Trigger.

D. Cursor.

8. Which of the following best describes an RDBMS?

   A. Database management system designed by Edgar F. Codd of IBM, which is based on the relational model.

   B. Database management system designed by Ken Thompson of IBM, which is based on the relational model.

   C. Database management system designed by Edgar F. Codd of Charles Babbage Institute, University of Minnesota, which is based on the relational model.

   D. Database management system designed by Dutch computer scientist, Edsger F. Codd of IBM, which is based on the relational model.

9. Which of the following best describes 1NF?

   A. Normal form used in database normalization, which, unlike other normal forms that are concerned with functional dependencies, is concerned with multivalued dependency.

   B. Property of a relation in a relational database that minimizes duplication of data by ensuring that no entry in a table is dependent on any other entry except the key.

   C. Property of a relation in a relational database, which involves keeping all attributes within an entity depending solely on the unique identifier of the entity.

   D. Property of a relation in a relational database, where first normal is a minimum requirement, and each column type is unique, with no group/type of data repeated.

10. When the property of a relation in a relational database minimizes data duplication by ensuring that no entry in a table is dependent on any other entry except the key. What is the NF?

    A. 2NF.

    B. 3NF.

    C. 4NF.

    D. 1NF.

11. What is the String data type?

    A. A sequence of characters that can either be any kind of variable, or a literal constant.

    B. A data type that represents some finite subset of the mathematical integers.

    C. A data type that can store values that have potential decimal places.

    D. Set of binary data stored in a database management

33

system as a single entity, primarily in the form of multimedia objects like audio, images, etc.

12. What is a non-relational and largely distributed database environment that allows for high-speed, ad-hoc analysis and organizing of high-volume data types called?

    A. SQL.
    B. MongoDB.
    C. Strozzi NoSQL.
    D. NoSQL.

13. When a clause is used on multiple tables to return a result as one table, based on a related column between the tables, what is this called?

    A. Join.
    B. View.
    C. Intersect.
    D. Union.

14. When sets of rules used are applied during the creation of a database, for the purposes of database normalization, what is the concept called?

    A. Forms.
    B. Recordset.
    C. Dataset.
    D. File objects.

15. What is a Foreign Key?

    A. Field in a database table that contains one or more columns whose combined values identify every row in a table uniquely.
    B. Field in a database table that is a unique identifier in the table.
    C. Field in a database table that refers to the primary key in another table.
    D. Field in a database table that refers to a combination of two or more columns in a table that uniquely identifies each row in the table.

16. Which of the following best describes Left Join?

    A. Operation that returns all the records from the table on the right, and only the matched records from the table on the left.
    B. Operation that returns all the records from the table on the left, and only the matched records from the table on the right.
    C. Operation where the resulting table retains all the rows even if there are no matching rows.
    D. Operation that returns only the records that have matching column values in both the tables.

17. When storage devices are located at various locations of a network, without being attached to a common processor, what is the database type called?

    A. Distributed Databases (DDB).
    B. Clustered Databases.
    C. Split Databases.
    D. Graph Databases.

18. How is a Table defined?

34

A. Set of data values corresponding to each row and column, defining the structure in which the schema is formed.

B. Set of data values in a relational database in the form of rows and columns, where a cell is the point of intersection between a row and a column.

C. Set of data values representing implicitly both structured and unstructured data items.

D. Collection of data, in the form of rows, columns, schemas, reports, queries, etc., arranged in a specific way.

19. What is the query command in SQL that allows you to assign the result of a query to a new private table?

A. Recordset.
B. Dataset.
C. View.
D. Dynaset.

20. What is an Outer Join?

A. Operation that returns all the records from the table on the right, and only the matched records from the table on the left.

B. Operation that returns all the records from the table on the left, and only the matched records from the table on the right.

C. Operation where the resulting table retains all the rows even if there are no matching rows.

D. Operation that returns only the records that have matching column values in both the tables.

21. What is a mechanism in RDBMS that protects the data integrity during server failures or when multiple users try to access the data at the same time?

A. Clustering.
B. Replication.
C. Transaction.
D. Creating Views.

22. How is Drop Table defined?

A. Statement used to delete a table definition, and all corresponding details including all the data, permission specifications, constraints, triggers, and indexes.

B. Statement used to delete a row in an existing table in a database. However, all records will be deleted if the 'WHERE' clause is not used with the Delete Row query.

C. Statement used to delete the data in a row of a table, you can choose to delete all the rows at once, or, choose a subset with the use of a condition.

D. Statement used to delete all rows from an existing table in a database.

23. A property that decides how transaction integrity is visible to other users, while ensuring that processes don't interfere with others. What is it called?

35

A. Durability.

B. Integrity.

C. Consistency.

D. Atomicity.

24. Which element allows users to decide how data is stored in a database, and how it is used?

    A. User-defined Data Type (UDT).

    B. Data Type.

    C. Recordset.

    D. Dataset.

25. Which of the following best describes Right Join?

    A. Operation where the resulting table retains all the rows even if there are no matching rows.

    B. Operation that returns only the records that have matching column values in both the tables.

    C. Operation that returns all the records from the table on the right, and only the matched records from the table on the left.

    D. Operation that returns all the records from the table on the left, and only the matched records from the table on the right.

26. What is clustering?

    A. Simplest way of optimizing an SQL database, where the contents of the database are organized in the same way as data is requested frequently.

    B. Operation where the resulting table retains all the rows even if there are no matching rows.

    C. Operation that returns all the records from the table on the right, and only the matched records from the table on the left.

    D. A type of lookup table that can be created for each column that is important, in order to optimize the performance of SQL databases.

27. Which of the following can be considered as a basic command in SQL?

    A. VIEW - for fetching and viewing data.

    B. MODIFY - for updating existing data.

    C. GROUP - for grouping data.

    D. INSERT - for inserting data.

28. What is the collection of data, in the form of tables, schemas, reports, queries, etc., arranged in a specific way, called?

    A. Database.

    B. Dataset.

    C. Data access objects.

    D. Recordset.

29. When a statement is used to insert a new row to an existing table in a database, what is the sequel command?

    A. Update Row.

    B. Select Row.

    C. Create Row.

    D. Insert Row.

30. You are looking at database normalization where a normal form involves keeping all attributes within an entity depending solely on the unique identifier of the entity. What is the NF?

    A. 1NF.
    B. 2NF.
    C. 3NF.
    D. 4NF.

31. What is SQL?

    A. Open-source relational framework based on Java, that is ideal for distributed storage and handling of very large amounts of data.
    B. Domain-specific language used primarily to manage data in a relational database management system, which uses a single command to access many records.
    C. A relational and non-relational, largely distributed database environment that allows for high-speed, ad-hoc analysis and organizing of high-volume data types.
    D. Domain-specific language including a family of algebras used for defining queries on relational databases, and modeling the data stored in them, giving a theoretical foundation.

32. Which of the following can be considered as a defining characteristic of a Procedural language?

    A. Easy to debug.
    B. Database-oriented.
    C. Fewer programming capabilities.
    D. File-oriented.

33. You are looking at the DBMS that supports modeling of data as objects, by integrating database capabilities with the capabilities of object-oriented programming languages. What is the DBMS called?

    A. RDBMS.
    B. ODBMS.
    C. RDS.
    D. BDBMS.

34. Which of the following best describes a Row?

    A. Collection of data items and schemas arranged in a specific way.
    B. Element that allows users to decide how data is stored in a database, and how it is used.
    C. Set of data values corresponding to each data item of the table, defining the structure.
    D. Field representing a single, implicitly structured data item in a table.

35. When the normal form separates semantically related multiple relationships, minimizes redundancies in relational databases that record multivalued facts, what is the NF?

    A. 2NF.

37

B. 5NF.

C. 4NF.

D. 3NF.

36. Which of the following best describes procedures?

    A. Subroutines that are written and stored in the database data dictionary and enable manipulation of entire result sets at once.

    B. Subroutines that are written only once and stored in the database data dictionary, and are available to any programming language that interacts with the database.

    C. Subroutines that are written as a set of SQL statements and are stored as a group in a relational database management system, and can be reused by multiple programs.

    D. Subroutines that are created by stored procedures, and other scripts, to reduce duplication while performing a specific task.

37. In the admission database, you want to add a new student table. What SQL statement is relevant in the context?

    A. CREATE TABLE student;

    B. INSERT TABLE student;

    C. UPDATE TABLE student;

    D. INSERT INTO student;

38. What is the Fourth Normal Form (4NF)?

    A. Property of a relation in a relational database that minimizes duplication of data by ensuring that no entry in a table is dependent on any other entry except the key.

    B. Property of a relation in a relational database, which involves keeping all attributes within an entity depending solely on the unique identifier of the entity.

    C. Property of a relation in a relational database, where first normal is a minimum requirement, and each column type is unique, with no group/type of data repeated.

    D. Normal form used in database normalization, which, unlike other normal forms that are concerned with functional dependencies, is concerned with multivalued dependency.

39. Which of the following best describes the integer data type?

    A. A data type that can store values that have potential decimal places.

    B. A data type that represents some finite subset of the mathematical integers.

    C. A data type that can store a date value.

    D. A data type that can store a point in time, including hours, minutes, seconds and usually, milliseconds.

40. Which of the following best describes the Consistency element in ACID properties?

    A. Property that requires a transaction to change affected data only in specifically allowed ways.
    B. Property that ensures that changes caused by a transaction survive permanently.
    C. Property that determines how transaction integrity is visible to other users, while ensuring that processes within one transaction cannot interfere with those in others.
    D. Property of a set of irreducible and indivisible set of database operations, considered as one operation, where either nothing occurs, or all occur.

41. What is the API used for DBMS access that is independent of operating systems and/or database systems called?

    A. SQL API.
    B. ODBC.
    C. JDBC.
    D. RDBC.

42. You have added a row in the student table in the admission database, but you wish to delete the row. Which of the following SQL command is relevant?

    A. Drop Row is a statement used to delete a row in an existing table in a database.
    B. Remove Row is a statement used to delete a row in an existing table in a database.
    C. Delete Row is a statement used to delete a row in an existing table in a database.
    D. Delete Column is a statement used to delete a row in an existing table in a database.

43. When a property of a set of irreducible and indivisible set of database operations are considered as one operation, where either nothing occurs, or all occur, what is the property called?

    A. Consistency.
    B. Durability.
    C. Integrity.
    D. Atomicity.

44. What is JDBC?

    A. API that is a SQL-level relational database connectivity targeting Scala and Java programming languages that is asynchronous to leverage Reactive Streams' stream processing capabilities.
    B. API used for DBMS access that is independent of operating systems and/or database systems.
    C. API used for Java database connectivity, that determines how a client using a Java run application can access the database.
    D. API used for PostgreSQL and Java database connectivity determining how to

perform complex queries or carrying out geospatial operations.

45. When a data type can store a value such as 01/01/2019, what is the data type?

    A. DateTime.
    B. String.
    C. Long Integer.
    D. Date.

46. Which of the following best describes an inner join?

    A. Operation that returns all the records from the table on the left, and only the matched records from the table on the right.
    B. Operation that returns all the records from the table on the right, and only the matched records from the table on the left.
    C. Operation that returns only the records that have matching column values in both the tables.
    D. Operation where the resulting table retains all the rows even if there are no matching rows.

47. The maximum temperature in October in Toronto was 13.4 degree Celsius. Which data type would be the best to store the value?

    A. Binary.
    B. Long Integer.
    C. Float.
    D. Integer.

48. What is the Durability property?

    A. Property that requires a transaction to change affected data only in specifically allowed ways.
    B. Property that determines how transaction integrity is visible to other users, while ensuring that processes within one transaction cannot interfere with those in others.
    C. Property of a set of irreducible and indivisible set of database operations, considered as one operation, where either nothing occurs, or all occur.
    D. Property that ensures that changes caused by a transaction survive permanently.

49. You want to store a set of binary data as a single entity, primarily in the form of multimedia objects like audio or images. What datatype should be used?

    A. String.
    B. User-defined Data Type (UDT).
    C. Binary.
    D. Blob.

5

NoSQL

1. Which of the following can be considered as a General Type of NoSQL Database?

   A. Clustered Database.
   B. Document Database.
   C. Distributed Database.
   D. Split Database.

2. Which of the following best describes a Cursor?

   A. Pointer to the results of single query having the potential to perform actions like creating, adding, retrieving, deleting, or updating records.
   B. Pointer indicating the direction to move and having the potential to access the same row in the result set multiple times.
   C. A data structure that consists of a group of database records, and can either come from a base table or as the result of a query to the table.
   D. Pointer to the results of a query that is returned for any query run, where clients can iterate through the cursor to retrieve documents.

3. Which of the following best describes Integrated Caching?

   A. Feature of NoSQL databases that provide automatic replication of data in order to maintain availability during maintenance events or outages.
   B. Feature that allows insertion of data into NoSQL databases without a predefined schema, enabling faster coding, more reliable code integration, and less admin time.
   C. Feature that spreads data across multiple servers, automatically balancing data and query load across servers, and replace servers without application disruption.
   D. Feature of NoSQL databases that minimize the need for separate

caching layers by storing frequently-used data in system memory to the maximum extent possible.

4. You want a Python distribution that offers tools to work with MongoDB, which is also a suggested distribution to work with MongoDB from Python. What is the distribution called?

   A. PyMongoORM.
   B. MongoDb.
   C. Real Python.
   D. PyMongo.

5. What is the feature that allows insertion of data into NoSQL databases without a predefined schema, enabling faster coding, more reliable code integration, and less admin time, called?

   A. Auto-sharding.
   B. Replication Schema.
   C. Integrated Caching.
   D. Dynamic Schema.

6. In NoSQL databases, data on one node could become out of sync with another node. What is this property called?

   A. Data Atomicity.
   B. Data Consistency.
   C. Data Integrity.
   D. Data Durability.

7. What is the name-value pair in a MongoDB document, which is much like a column in a relational DB, called?

   A. Collection.
   B. Field.

   C. RowSet.
   D. Document.

8. Which of the following database transaction properties is provided by a BASE system?

   A. Soft-state.
   B. Atomicity.
   C. Durability.
   D. Auto-sharding.

9. Which of the following best describes Real Location Independence?

   A. NoSQL allows one or more servers or nodes to continue operating without any loss of data when one or more servers or nodes go down.
   B. NoSQL allows immediate or eventual consistency of data across all nodes that participate in a distributed database based on the changing architecture.
   C. NoSQL allows read and write operations, irrespective of where the operation occurs physically, making the database available to users at multiple locations.
   D. NoSQL allows housing of all types of data, even those without a schema like structured, semi-structured, and unstructured data.

10. What is a non-relational and largely distributed database environment that allows for high-speed, ad-hoc analysis and organizing of high-volume data types?

42

A. SQL.

B. MongoDB.

C. Strozzi NoSQL.

D. NoSQL.

11. You are looking at a data storage and network transfer format used in MongoDB, which is a binary variant for representing MongoDB documents in different data types. What is the format called?

    A. MessagePack.

    B. JSON.

    C. YAML.

    D. BSON.

12. What is the mandatory field for every MongoDB document that represents a unique value, and acts as the primary key of the document called?

    A. key_part_id.

    B. _id.

    C. key_one.

    D. utc_id.

13. Which of the following best describes Riak?

    A. An open-source, NoSQL, distributed, column-oriented data store built on HDFS that offers horizontal scaling and random real-time read/write access to data on Hadoop.

    B. A distributed NoSQL key-value data store that fault-tolerant, highly available, and easily scalable.

    C. An open-source, NoSQL, distributed data store that offers high availability, and handles large data sets across many commodity servers.

    D. An open-source, NoSQL, document-oriented data store software that uses JSON for data storage.

14. What is DynamoDB?

    A. An open-source, NoSQL, embedded software library that supports multiple data items for a single key, and offers a high-performance, scalable, database.

    B. An open-source, NoSQL, distributed database service that offers high availability, and handles large data sets across many commodity servers with no single point of failure.

    C. A proprietary, NoSQL database service that offers high availability, scalability, and durability, and uses synchronous replication across various data centers.

    D. An open-source, NoSQL, distributed, column-oriented database service built on HDFS, that offers horizontal scaling and random real-time read/write access to data on Hadoop.

15. When an open-source, in-memory database management system supports many abstract data structures like strings, hyperlog logs, etc., and offers

durability, what is the system called?

A. Redis.
B. Hbase.
C. DynamoDB.
D. Cassandra.

16. When the most recent write, or an error, for every read is guaranteed, and all servers have the same data to ensure uniform query results, what is the concept called?

    A. Replication.
    B. Integrated Caching.
    C. Auto-sharding.
    D. Consistency.

17. You are looking at a data storage that has an undetermined number of relations, all of which are represented as a graph, with interconnected elements. What type of NoSQL database is this?

    A. Column Store.
    B. Graph Database.
    C. Key-Value Store.
    D. Document Databases.

18. You are looking at an open-source, NoSQL, cross-platform database that is document oriented, and uses documents similar to JSON with schemas. What is the database called?

    A. CouchDB.
    B. DynamoDB.
    C. Berkeley DB.
    D. MongoDB.

19. What is a Collection?

    A. The grouping of documents in MongoDB, like tables in other RDBMS services, which don't require any kind of structure.
    B. The grouping of documents in Berkeley DB, like tables in other ORDBMS services, which require similar kind of structure.
    C. The grouping of individual records saved in a MongoDB, which stores data in the form of field names and values.
    D. The container in which data is stored on MongoDB, with its own set of files on the file system.

20. What is Replication?

    A. Feature that spreads data across multiple servers, automatically balancing data and query load across servers, and replace servers without application disruption.
    B. Feature that allows insertion of data into NoSQL databases without a predefined schema, enabling faster coding, more reliable code integration, and less admin time.
    C. Feature of NoSQL databases that provide automatic replication of data in order to maintain availability during maintenance events or outages.
    D. Feature of NoSQL databases that minimize the need for separate

44

caching layers by storing frequently-used data in system memory to the maximum extent possible.

21. What is the feature that spreads data across multiple servers, automatically balancing data and query load across servers, and replacing servers without application disruption, called?

    A. Integrated Caching.
    B. Dynamic Schema.
    C. Auto-sharding.
    D. Replication Schema.

22. What is a Document?

    A. Name-value pair in a MongoDB, which is much like a column in a relational DB.
    B. The container in which collections are stored on MongoDB, with its own set of files on the file system.
    C. Individual records saved in a MongoDB collection, which store data in the form of field names and values.
    D. Single record saved in a MongoDB collection, which stores data in the form of unique identifiers and values.

23. Which of the following best describes Giraph?

    A. A distributed NoSQL key-value data store that fault-tolerant, highly available, and easily scalable.
    B. An iterative database system designed for high scalability and graph processing on big data that uses Hadoop MapReduce implementation.
    C. A proprietary, NoSQL database service that offers high availability, scalability, and durability, and uses synchronous replication across various data centers.
    D. An open-source, NoSQL, distributed, column-oriented database built on HDFS that offers horizontal scaling and random real-time read/write access to data on Hadoop.

24. Which of the following best describes Lack of Standardization in NoSQL?

    A. As the NoSQL community is not as well defined as the user bases of relational databases, and is still growing, NoSQL users might face lack of support.
    B. As most NoSQL databases rely on eventual consistency, and do not perform all ACID transactions, data on one node can go out of sync with that on another node.
    C. As NoSQL does not support a standard query language, it could cause issues during migration of databases from other environments.
    D. As NoSQL focuses on scalability and performance, the

45

environments tend to offer relatively less data security as compared to relational databases.

25. Which of the following best describes Partition Tolerance?

    A. Guarantees the most recent write, or an error, for every read. This also means that all servers will have the same data to ensure uniform query results.

    B. Guarantees a non-error response to every request, whether or not it includes the most recent write.

    C. Guarantees continuous operation of the system as a whole, regardless of any messages being delayed or dropped between nodes, or any failure of individual servers.

    D. Feature of NoSQL databases that provide automatic replication of data in order to maintain availability during maintenance events or outages.

26. When each key is paired with a document, which is nothing but a complex data structure that may have several key-value pairs, or nested documents, what is the concept called?

    A. Document Databases.

    B. Key-Value Store.

    C. Column Store.

    D. Graph Database.

27. What is Continuous Data Availability?

    A. In NoSQL databases, if one is offered immediate or eventual consistency of data across all nodes that participate in a distributed database based on the changing architecture.

    B. In NoSQL databases, if one or more servers focus on scalability and performance, and environments tend to offer relatively less data security as compared to relational databases.

    C. In NoSQL databases, if one is allowed read and write operations, irrespective of where the operation occurs physically, making the database available to users at multiple locations.

    D. In NoSQL databases, if one or more servers or nodes go down, other servers and nodes can continue operating without any loss of data.

28. You are looking at a container in which collections are stored on MongoDB, with its own set of files on the file system. What is the concept called?

    A. Collection.

    B. DataSet.

    C. Document.

    D. Database.

29. What is Hbase?

    A. An open-source, NoSQL, cross-platform database, that is document oriented, and uses documents similar to JSON with schemas.

46

B. An open-source, NoSQL, distributed, column-oriented database built on HDFS, that offers horizontal scaling and random real-time read/write access to data on Hadoop.

C. An open-source, NoSQL, distributed database that offers high availability, and handles large data sets across many commodity servers with no single point of failure.

D. An open-source, NoSQL, document-oriented database software that uses JSON for data storage, and aims at providing scalability and ease of use.

30. You are looking at a distributed data store that can only provide two of these three guarantees at a time: Consistency, Availability, and Partition Tolerance. What is the concept called?

A. Auto-sharding.

B. CAP Theorem.

C. Integrated Caching.

D. Dynamic Schema.

31. You are looking at an open-source, NoSQL, distributed database that handles large data sets across many commodity servers with no single point of failure. What is the database called?

A. DynamoDB.

B. Cassandra.

C. Hbase.

D. Redis.

32. Which of the following best describes JavaScript Object Notation?

A. Data format for expressing structured data in a plain text, human readable form, and is supported in several programming languages.

B. Data format for expressing unstructured data in a unicode form, and is supported in visual programming languages.

C. Python distribution that offers tools to work with MongoDB, which is also the most widely suggested distribution to work with MongoDB from Python.

D. Data storage and network transfer format used in MongoDB, which is a binary variant for representing MongoDB documents in different data types.

33. What is Availability?

A. Guarantees the most recent write, or an error, for every read. This also means that all servers will have the same data to ensure uniform query results.

B. Guarantees a non-error response to every request, whether or not it includes the most recent write.

C. Feature of NoSQL databases that provide automatic replication of data in order to maintain availability during maintenance events or outages.

D. Guarantees continuous operation of the system as a whole, regardless of any messages being delayed or dropped between nodes, or any failure of individual servers.

34. You want to know more about the elements to be considered before choosing a NoSQL database. Which of the following is a relevant element most specific to NoSQL?

    A. Integrity.
    B. Scalability.
    C. Atomicity.
    D. Durability.

35. What is Neo4J?

    A. An open-source, NoSQL, document-oriented database software that uses JSON for data storage, and aims at providing scalability and ease of use.
    B. An open-source, NoSQL, distributed database that offers high availability, and handles large data sets across many commodity servers with no single point of failure.
    C. An open-source, NoSQL, ACID-compliant graph database management system, that provides native graph storage and processing.
    D. An open-source, NoSQL, cross-platform database, that is document oriented, and uses documents similar to JSON with schemas.

36. When data tables are stored together, as sections of columns of data, instead of rows, providing a high performing scalable design for large datasets, what is the concept called?

    A. Data column stores.
    B. Wide Rowsets.
    C. Data Rowsets.
    D. Wide column stores.

37. What is a Flexible Data Model?

    A. NoSQL databases can have a flexible schema that supports user customization and allows users to declare new fields on demand.
    B. NoSQL databases can describe the structure of data irrespective of the stored form and is built on the Entity-Relationship Model.
    C. NoSQL databases are a part of an open source object-relational mapping framework and can bind an object to its data in the database.
    D. NoSQL databases can house all types of data, even those without a schema like structured, semi-structured, and unstructured data.

38. Which of the following is an element to be considered before choosing a NoSQL database?

    A. Performance.
    B. Durability.
    C. Atomicity.
    D. Integrity.

39. You are looking at an open-source, NoSQL, document-oriented database software that uses JSON for data storage, and aims at providing scalability. What is the database called?

    A. MySQL.
    B. Hive.
    C. Pig.
    D. CouchDB.

40. Which of the following best describes Berkeley DB?

    A. An open-source, NoSQL, document-oriented database software that uses JSON for data storage, and aims at providing scalability and ease of use.
    B. An open-source, NoSQL, distributed database that offers high availability, and handles large data sets across many commodity servers with no single point of failure.
    C. An open-source, NoSQL, distributed, column-oriented database built on HDFS that offers horizontal scaling and random real-time read/write access to data on Hadoop.
    D. An open-source, NoSQL, embedded software library that supports multiple data items for a single key, and offers a high-performance, scalable, database.

41. What is a Key Value store?

    A. Store data that has an undetermined number of relations, all of which are represented as a graph, with interconnected elements.
    B. Pair each key with a document, which is nothing but a complex data structure that may have several key-value pairs, or key-array pairs, or nested documents.
    C. Store data tables together, as sections of columns of data, instead of rows, providing a high performing scalable design for large datasets.
    D. Store data in a schema-less manner, where each item is stored along with its value, in the form of an indexed key (or an attribute name).

6

Hadoop

1. Built on Hadoop YARN, which extesible framework enables building of high-performance data processing applications?

    A. Apache Ambari.
    B. Apache Mahout.
    C. Apache Tez.
    D. Apache Pig.

2. Which software platform that runs on Apache Hadoop, helps build programs, and executes Hadoop jobs?

    A. Apache Zookeeper.
    B. Apache Ambari.
    C. Apache Pig.
    D. Apache Mahout.

3. Which of the following best describes Apache Hive?

    A. A data warehouse software built on Hadoop, that offers data summarization, query, and analysis for large data sets, and uses SQL as it's query language.

    B. Open-source distributed computing platform for provisioning, managing, and monitoring Hadoop clusters, and integrating existing enterprise infrastructure with Hadoop.

    C. Library of distributed machine-learning algorithms in areas of classification, clustering, and collaborative filtering, implemented using MapReduce, on Hadoop.

    D. Software platform that runs on Apache Hadoop, and helps build programs, analyze large data sets, and execute Hadoop jobs in Apache Tez, MapReduce, etc.

4. What is Hadoop?

    A. Highly extensible programming language that offers a many graphical and statistical techniques, used primarily in data analysis and statistical software.

B. An object-oriented, interpreted, high-level programming language that offers code readability, and constructs for writing large and small scale programs clearly.

C. Applied field in Artificial Intelligence that focuses on training computer programs with algorithms that allow them to learn without being specifically programmed.

D. Open-source software framework based on Java, that is ideal for distributed storage and handling of very large amounts of data.

5. Which of the following best describes Apache Zookeeper?

A. Library of distributed machine-learning algorithms in areas of classification, clustering, and collaborative filtering, implemented using MapReduce, on Hadoop.

B. Open-source distributed computing platform for provisioning, managing, and monitoring Hadoop clusters, and integrating existing enterprise infrastructure with Hadoop.

C. A cross-platform service that offers a key-value store for distributed configuration, synchronization, and naming registry services for large systems.

D. Software platform that runs on Apache Hadoop, and helps build programs, analyze large data sets, and execute Hadoop jobs in Apache Tez, MapReduce, etc.

6. What is Apache Ambari?

A. Software platform that runs on Apache Hadoop, and helps build programs, analyze large data sets, and execute Hadoop jobs in Apache Tez, MapReduce, etc.

B. Open-source distributed computing platform for provisioning, managing, and monitoring Hadoop clusters, and integrating existing enterprise infrastructure with Hadoop.

C. A cross-platform service that offers a key-value store for distributed configuration, synchronization, and naming registry services for large systems.

D. Library of distributed machine-learning algorithms in areas of classification, clustering, and collaborative filtering, implemented using MapReduce, on Hadoop.

7. What is an open-source framework for cluster-computing that offers an interface for programming entire clusters with fault-tolerance, and implicit data-parallelism, called?

A. Apache Tez.

B. Apache Spark.

C. Apache Mahout.

D. Apache Pig.

8. What is the Library of distributed machine-learning algorithms in areas of classification, clustering, and collaborative filtering, implemented using MapReduce, on Hadoop, called?

   A. Apache Mahout.
   B. Apache Zookeeper.
   C. Apache Ambari.
   D. Apache Pig.

9. What is the Primary component of the Apache Hadoop framework, which is a programming model used for distributed computing of large amounts of data on a cluster, called?

   A. HDFS.
   B. MapReduce.
   C. Ambari.
   D. Mahout.

10. Which of the following is NOT a common Hadoop input format?

    A. Text.
    B. Key-Value.
    C. Hash.
    D. Sequence Input.

11. Which of the following is true in Hadoop, compared to an RDBMS?

    A. Reads are faster.
    B. Writes are faster.
    C. Both reads and writes are faster.
    D. Both reads and writes are the same.

7

Machine Learning

1. Which statistical model relates a set of manifest variables to a set of latent variables?

   A. Hidden Variable Model.
   B. SVM Model.
   C. Hidden Markov Model.
   D. Mixture Model.

2. Which of the following can be considered as a weakness of Bayesian classifier?

   A. Not equipped to handle permutations that can't change due to dynamic features.
   B. Not equipped to handle outcomes that change due to combinations of features.
   C. Classifier cannot draw out combinations as features are given permutations.
   D. Classifier cannot match combinations as the algorithm is a given representation of probability distribution.

3. What is Kernel Density Estimation?

   A. Technique that estimates the parameter values that maximize the likelihood of making the observations, for a given statistical model.
   B. A non-parametric method of estimating the probability density function of a random variable, where a finite data sample is used to make inferences about the population.
   C. Technique that estimates population parameters by deriving equations that relate the population moments to the parameters of interest.
   D. Technique that on the basis on empirical data, estimates an unknown quantity that equals the mode of the posterior distribution.

4. What is the technique that estimates the parameter values that maximize the likelihood of making the observations, for a given statistical model, called?

A. Kernel Density Estimation.

B. MAP Estimation.

C. MLE Estimation.

D. MOM Estimation.

5. Which of the following best describes Supervised Learning?

   A. Applications don't receive any training with examples, but learn by finding structure within a given set of data to recognize groups that exist within them.

   B. Applications learn to make predictions by first looking at example sets of inputs and outputs, and then applying this learning to a given task.

   C. Applications are an approach to rule learning that uses logic programming as a uniform representation for input examples and hypotheses.

   D. Applications that use a decision tree as a predictive model and maps observations to the item's target value.

6. Which of the following can be best described as a Feature Vector?

   A. A vector of numerical features, with n-dimension, representing objects and enabling statistical analysis.

   B. A vector that works around each word towards a model that can differentiate between real words and noise words.

   C. A vector that is an eigenvector and a phenomenon having independent properties of magnitude and direction.

   D. A vector that constructs a hyperplane or a set of hyperplanes in a high dimensional space and can be used for regression and other tasks.

7. You are looking at an approach that can turn a linear model into a nonlinear model by replacing its predictors by a kernel function. What is the concept called?

   A. LIBSVM Kernel Optimization.

   B. The Kernel Transformation.

   C. The Kernel Trick.

   D. Radial Basis Function.

8. Which of the following can be best described as Simulated Annealing?

   A. Technique that, on the basis on empirical data, estimates an unknown quantity that equals the mode of the posterior distribution.

   B. Chooses the strongest solution among a pool of random solutions, which is the one with the lowest cost, through modification and trait combination techniques.

   C. Predicts the global optimum of a function by predicting a random solution at first, and improving the

56

same by determining the cost of another random solution.

D. Method of using optimization algorithms to select values that minimize the output of a cost function.

9. What is a set of data that is used to find possible predictive relationships, called?

   A. Data Set.
   B. Test Set.
   C. Recommender Systems.
   D. Training Set.

10. What is the generative graphical architecture composed of multiple layers of hidden variables where the layers are connected, but not the units between them, called?

    A. Recurrent Neural Networks.
    B. Convolutional Neural Networks (CNN).
    C. Deep Feedforward Networks.
    D. Deep Belief Network.

11. Which of the following can be considered as a Common Deep Learning Software Library?

    A. LibSVM.
    B. KStar.
    C. Lasagne.
    D. SPegasos.

12. What is Cosine Similarity?

    A. Model in NLP for large sets of discrete data like text corpora, which lets sets of observations to be explained for their similarity in data, by unobserved groups.
    B. Technique used to find a two-dimensional representation of a dataset that visualizes the level of similarity of individual cases.
    C. Measure of similarity, where a few support vectors or critical boundary instances are chosen from each class, to build a linear discriminant function.
    D. Measure of similarity between 2 non-zero vectors of an inner product space, or two documents on the Vector Space, that computes the cosine of the angle between them.

13. You are looking at directed and acyclic graphs that help keep track of how complicated computations decompose. What is the graph called?

    A. PyTorch.
    B. Pseudographs.
    C. Computation Graphs.
    D. Static Graphs.

14. Which of the following best describes Caffe?

    A. An open-source deep learning framework written in JVM and Java, that supports a wide range of deep learning algorithms.
    B. An open-source deep learning framework written with a Python interface,

in C++, primarily supporting image segmentation and image classification.

C. An open-source neural network framework written in Python, and designed to be minimal, extensible, and modular, and aid fast experimentation with deep neural networks.

D. An open-source script language and machine learning library based on the Lua programming language, that offers several algorithms for deep learning.

15. Which of the following best describes Principal Component Analysis?

A. The approach of turning any linear model into a non-linear model by replacing its predictors by a kernel function.

B. Procedure in an artificial neural network that converts the inputs into something that can be used by the output layer.

C. An unsupervised learning model, where a few support vectors or critical boundary instances are chosen from each class, to build a linear discriminant function.

D. Procedure that converts observations of possibly correlated variables into values of linearly uncorrelated variables, using an orthogonal transformation.

16. What is Forward Propagation?

A. A Markov process that has either discrete index set, or discrete state space, usually representing time.

B. Process of multiplying input with weights, and adding bias prior to applying activation function at each node.

C. Process of using a specific value, or set of values, and deriving the probability of one or more random variables.

D. Process of increasing the number of data points, and in turn the data size to be fed to machine learning classifiers, that saves cost and time in data collection.

17. You are looking at a meta-algorithm that improves the accuracy of machine learning algorithms by combining predictions through methods of averaging. What is the concept called?

A. Blending.

B. Bagging.

C. Randomization.

D. Boosting.

18. Which of the following best describes a Boltzmann Machine?

A. A type of stochastic Markov random field, used usually for unsupervised learning, where units correspond to random variables.

B. Meta-algorithm that improves the accuracy and

58

stability of machine learning algorithms by combining predictions through methods of averaging or voting.

C. A stochastic neural network that learns a probability distribution over a set of inputs, only with the restriction that its neurons should form a bipartite graph.

D. A type of binary pairwise Markov random field involving coupling layers of hidden random variables, using RBM connectivity.

19. What is the technique that on the basis on empirical data, estimates an unknown quantity that equals the mode of the posterior distribution, called?

    A. MOM Estimation.
    B. Kernel Density Estimation.
    C. MAP Estimation.
    D. MLE Estimation.

20. What is the applied field in Artificial Intelligence that focuses on training computer programs with algorithms that allow them to learn without being specifically programmed, called?

    A. Machine Learning.
    B. Unsupervised Learning.
    C. Supervised Learning.
    D. Decision Tree Learning.

21. Which of the following best describes Latent Dirichlet Allocation?

    A. Model in NLP for large sets of discrete data like text corpora, which lets sets of observations to be explained for their similarity in data, by unobserved groups.
    B. Procedure in NLP that converts observations of possibly correlated variables into values of linearly uncorrelated variables, using an orthogonal transformation.
    C. Type of stochastic Markov random field, used usually for NLP, where units correspond to random variables.
    D. Technique in NLP that analyzes relationships between a set of documents and their terms, by creating a set of concepts related to the documents and terms.

22. You are looking at autoencoders that can learn low-dimensional representations using the same number of dimensions, with lesser reconstruction error than PCA. What are they called?

    A. Deep Learning.
    B. Deep Autoencoders.
    C. Data Augmentation.
    D. Hyperparameter Tuning.

23. What is the type of binary pairwise Markov random field involving coupling layers of hidden random variables, using RBM connectivity, called?

    A. Support Vector Machines.
    B. Restricted Boltzmann Machine (RBM).

C. Convolutional Neural Network Machine (CNN)

D. Deep RBM (Restricted Boltzmann Machine).

24. What is an adjoining sequence of n items from a specified sequence of speech or text, like syllables, base, pairs, phonemes, etc., called?

    A. Recommender Systems.
    B. k-means.
    C. n-gram.
    D. Recurrent Neural Networks.

25. What is the layer in an artificial neural network that converts the inputs into something that can be used by the output layer, called?

    A. Masked Layer.
    B. Hidden Layer.
    C. Activation Layer.
    D. Latent Semantic Layer.

26. You are looking at an algorithm that is used for supervised learning of binary classifiers, which processes elements in the training set one at a time. What is the algorithm called?

    A. Gibbs Sampling.
    B. Perceptron.
    C. Data Augmentation.
    D. Probabilistic Inference.

27. What is the representation of the set of all hierarchical trees of a specific data set that helps better understanding of hierarchical clusterings, called?

    A. Option Tree.
    B. Alternating Decision Trees.
    C. DensiTree.
    D. Decision Tree.

28. Which of the following best describes Bias-Variance Decomposition?

    A. Method of using many diverse models in order to compute the initial prediction and mixing predictions to achieve a better final prediction.
    B. Method of training an algorithm to combine the predictions of multiple models or algorithms as additional inputs to the already available data.
    C. Method of analyzing an algorithm's expected generalization error as the sum of the bias, variance, and the irreducible error.
    D. Method of using optimization algorithms to select values that minimize the output of a cost function.

29. What is Lasagne?

    A. An open-source neural network framework written in Python, and designed to be minimal, extensible, and modular, and aid fast experimentation with deep neural networks.
    B. An open-source deep learning framework written with a Python interface, in C++, primarily supporting image segmentation and image classification.

C. An open-source software library for JVM and Java, that supports a wide range of deep learning algorithms.

D. A lightweight software library that helps build and train neural networks on Theano, which supports feed-forward networks, and offers freely definable cost function.

30. What is the function of a node that determines the output of that specific node, given an input or a set of inputs, called?

   A. The Cost Function.
   B. Hidden Function.
   C. Activation Function.
   D. Latent Semantic Function.

31. What is Hyperparameter Tuning?

   A. The challenge of selecting a set of optimal hyperparameters for a learning algorithm that maximizes the algorithm's performance.
   B. The challenge of selecting a structure and function inspired by the function of the human brain that maximizes the algorithm's tasks.
   C. The challenge of detecting and deciphering patterns and correlations for a learning algorithm that maximizes the human reasoning.
   D. The challenge of selecting a set of optional spatial structures for a learning algo-

rithm that maximizes digit recognition.

32. What is MOM Estimation?

   A. Technique that estimates the parameter values that maximize the likelihood of making the observations, for a given statistical model.
   B. Technique that, on the basis on empirical data, estimates an unknown quantity that equals the mode of the posterior distribution.
   C. A non-parametric method of estimating the probability density function of a random variable, where a finite data sample is used to make inferences about the population.
   D. Technique that estimates population parameters by deriving equations that relate the population moments to the parameters of interest.

33. What are Convolutional Neural Networks (CNN)?

   A. A type of neural network where the hidden units are not random variables, hence the connections between the units do not form a cycle.
   B. Neural networks that have an internal state, as the connections between their units form a directed cycle. Can handle learning problems concerning sequences of data.

61

C. A class of deep feedforward neural networks used for image analysis as it is capable of learning both the classifier, and the filter using backpropagation and SGD.

D. A generative graphical architecture composed of multiple layers of hidden variables where the layers are connected, but not the units between them.

34. You are looking at a function that predicts a solution that is lower for solutions that are better for those that are worse than the one in context. What is the concept called?

    A. Probability Function.
    B. Optimization.
    C. The Cost Function.
    D. Simulated Annealing.

35. What are computing systems that are inspired by the design and functioning of the biological networks in animal brains, called?

    A. Deep Belief Network.
    B. Convolutional Neural Networks (CNN).
    C. Neural Networks.
    D. Deep Feedforward Networks.

36. What is Naive Bayes?

    A. An ensemble learning meta-algorithm that uses intuitive justification and an iterative model to reduce bias and variance in supervised learning.

    B. Set of probabilistic classifiers that apply Bayes' theorem with naive independence assumptions between features, and use normal distribution to model numeric attributes.

    C. A supervised learning model, where a few support vectors or critical boundary instances are chosen from each class, to build a linear discriminant function.

    D. Statistical model of representing probability distributions in a graphical way, drawn out as a network of nodes connected by directed edges, as an acyclic graph.

37. Which of the following best describes Alternating Decision Trees?

    A. Decision trees with option nodes where predictions from different branches are merged either by averaging probability estimates or by voting.

    B. A representation of the set of all hierarchical trees of a specific data set, that helps better understanding of hierarchical clusterings.

    C. Predictive machine learning method that adopts a transparent way of classifying observations, and sequencing what look like a set of if-then statements, into a tree.

    D. Type of option tree where nodes are added incrementally using a boosting algorithm, and has splitter nodes and prediction nodes.

38. You are looking at decision trees with option nodes where predictions from different branches are merged by averaging probability estimates or by voting. What is the concept called?

    A. Alternating Decision Trees.
    B. Hierarchical Clustering.
    C. Option Trees.
    D. DensiTree.

39. What is the clustering algorithm that reduces distance from all points to their cluster centers, and is instructed in advance to generate a specific number of clusters (k), called?

    A. Convolutional Neural Networks (CNN).
    B. k-means.
    C. DensiTree.
    D. Hierarchical Clustering.

40. What is Boosting?

    A. Meta-algorithm used to generate samples from a joint distribution even when the true distribution is a complex continuous function.
    B. An ensemble learning meta-algorithm that uses intuitive justification and an iterative model to reduce bias and variance in supervised learning.
    C. Meta-algorithm that improves the accuracy and stability of machine learning algorithms by combining predictions through methods of averaging or voting.
    D. Algorithm for class probability estimation, which can get an algorithm for classification by using additive regression alongside logit transformation.

41. What is Backpropagation?

    A. Iterative optimization algorithm that goes with the negative of the gradient, to find the local minimum of a function, when the objective function is differentiable.
    B. Algorithm used in artificial neural networks for supervised learning, that calculates the error contribution of each neuron after a data batch is processed.
    C. Algorithm used to generate samples from a joint distribution even when the true distribution is a complex continuous function in artificial neural networks.
    D. Algorithm used in artificial neural networks to automatically predict the preferences of a smaller set of users by collecting those of many users.

42. Which of the following can be considered as a Step of EM Algorithm?

A. E-Step: Calculates the expectations used in the expected log-likelihood.

B. E-Step: Maximizes the objective via a closed-form parameter update.

C. O-Step: Calculates the expectations used in the expected log-likelihood.

D. M-Step: Maximizes the objective via a closed-form parameter update.

43. What is cuDNN?

A. An open-source script language and machine learning library based on the Lua programming language, that offers several algorithms for deep learning.

B. A GPU-accelerated deep neural network library by NVIDIA, designed to offer highly tuned implementations for routines like pooling, convolution, normalization, etc.

C. A lightweight software library that helps build and train neural networks on Theano, which supports feed-forward networks, and offers freely definable cost function.

D. An open-source software library for JVM and Java, that supports a wide range of deep learning algorithms.

44. Which of the following best describes data augmentation?

A. Process of using a specific value, or set of values, and deriving the probability of one or more random variables.

B. Technique used to find a two-dimensional representation of a dataset that visualizes the level of similarity of individual cases.

C. Process of increasing the number of data points, and in turn the data size to be fed to machine learning classifiers, that saves cost and time in data collection.

D. Method of training an algorithm to combine the predictions of multiple models or algorithms as additional inputs to the already available data.

45. Which ensemble learning method constructs several decision trees during training, and results in the mean prediction of the classes?

A. Additive Regression.

B. Random Forest.

C. Option Trees.

D. Boosting.

46. You are looking at a process that uses a specific value, or set of values, and derives the probability of one or more random variables. What is the concept called?

A. Sampling.

B. Gibbs Sampling.

C. Data Augmentation.

D. Probabilistic Inference.

47. What is Keras?

64

A. An open-source deep learning framework written with a Python interface, in C++, primarily supporting image segmentation and image classification.

B. A lightweight software library that helps build and train neural networks on Theano, which supports feed-forward networks, and offers freely definable cost function.

C. An open-source software library for JVM and Java, that supports a wide range of deep learning algorithms.

D. An open-source neural network library written in Python, and designed to be minimal, extensible, and modular, and aid fast experimentation with deep neural networks.

48. Which of the following best describes Autoencoders?

A. A machine learning method based on learning data representation, instead of the traditional task-specific algorithms.

B. A neural network used for unsupervised learning, that is capable of learning efficient coding by learning representation of a data set for dimensionality reduction.

C. Neural networks that have an internal state, as the connections between their units form a directed cycle, and can handle learning problems concerning sequences of data.

D. A stochastic neural network that learns a probability distribution over a set of inputs, only with the restriction that its neurons should form a bipartite graph.

49. When an algorithm is used to generate samples from a joint distribution even when the true distribution is a complex continuous function, what is the concept called?

A. Data Augmentation.

B. Gibbs Sampling.

C. Probabilistic Inference.

D. Hyperparameter Tuning

50. What is Multidimensional Scaling?

A. Technique used to find a two-dimensional representation of a dataset that visualizes the level of similarity of individual cases.

B. Technique that estimates population parameters by deriving equations that relate the population moments to the parameters of interest.

C. Technique that on the basis on empirical data, estimates an unknown quantity that equals the mode of the posterior distribution.

D. Technique that estimates the parameter values that maximize the likelihood of making the observations, for a given statistical model.

51. What is a Genetic Algorithm?

    A. Method of using optimization algorithms to select values that minimize the output of a cost function.
    B. Predicts the global optimum of a function by predicting a random solution at first, and improving the same by determining the cost of another random solution.
    C. Technique that, on the basis on empirical data, estimates an unknown quantity that equals the mode of the posterior distribution.
    D. Chooses the strongest solution among a pool of random solutions, which is the one with the lowest cost, through modification and trait combination techniques.

52. What is the algorithm used by recommender systems to automatically predict the preferences of a smaller set of users by collecting those of many users, called?

    A. Attribute Filtering.
    B. Collaborative Filtering.
    C. Bayesian Filtering.
    D. Document Filtering.

53. Which of the following best describes Stacking?

    A. An ensemble learning meta-algorithm that uses intuitive justification and an iterative model to reduce bias and variance in supervised learning.
    B. Meta-algorithm that improves the accuracy and stability of machine learning algorithms by combining predictions through methods of averaging or voting.
    C. Method of using many diverse models in order to compute the initial prediction and mixing predictions to achieve a better final prediction.
    D. Method of training an algorithm to combine the predictions of multiple models or algorithms as additional inputs to the already available data.

54. You are looking at ways of implementation in deep learning in Weka. Which of the following can be considered as a relevant way?

    A. Using the multi-layer perceptron classifiers available in the third-party Caffe package.
    B. Accessing .Net-based deep learning libraries through the NuGet package.
    C. Exploiting deep learning implementations for R with the use of RBFClassifier from the VIM Plugin Manager.
    D. Exploiting deep learning implementations for R with the use of MLRClassifier from the RPlugin package.

55. What is an open-source software library for JVM and Java, that supports a wide range

66

of deep learning algorithms, called?

A. Deeplearning4j.

B. Torch.

C. Lasagne.

D. Caffe.

56. What is Unsupervised Learning?

A. Applications that use a decision tree as a predictive model and maps observations to the item's target value.

B. Applications don't receive any training with examples, but learn by finding structure within a given set of data to recognize groups that exist within them.

C. Applications are an approach to rule learning that uses logic programming as a uniform representation for input examples and hypotheses.

D. Applications learn to make predictions by first looking at example sets of inputs and outputs, and then applying this learning to a given task.

57. You want to know more about the weakness of Bayesian classifier. Which of the following can be considered as a weakness?

A. Classifier cannot draw out combinations as features are given permutations.

B. Classifier cannot match combinations as the algorithm is a given representation of probability distribution.

C. Classifier cannot learn about combinations as features are given probabilities individually.

D. Not equipped to handle permutations that can't change due to dynamic features.

58. What is the type of regularization used while training a learner with an iterative method, in order to prevent overfitting, called?

A. Stopping Evolution.

B. Genetic Optimization Stopping.

C. Annealing Starting.

D. Early Stopping.

59. You are looking at neural networks that have an internal state, as the connections between their units form a directed cycle. What are they called?

A. Convolutional Neural Networks (CNN).

B. Deep Belief Network.

C. Deep Feedforward Networks.

D. Recurrent Neural Networks.

60. What is a Support Vector Machine?

A. An ensemble learning meta-algorithm that uses

intuitive justification and an iterative model to reduce bias and variance in supervised learning.

B. A supervised learning model, where a few support vectors or critical boundary instances are chosen from each class, to build a linear discriminant function.

C. Predictive machine learning method that adopts a transparent way of classifying observations, and sequencing what look like a set of if-then statements, into a tree.

D. An ensemble learning method that constructs several decision trees during training, and results in either the mean prediction, or the mode of the classes.

61. What is Hierarchical Clustering?

A. A cluster analysis technique that builds a hierarchy of groups by constantly merging the two groups that are most similar.

B. A representation of the set of all hierarchical trees of a specific data set, that helps better understanding of hierarchical clusterings.

C. A class of cluster feedforward neural networks used for image analysis as it is capable of learning both the classifier, and the filter using backpropagation and SGD.

D. Clustering algorithm that reduces distance from all points to their cluster centers, and is instructed in advance to generate a specific number of clusters (k).

62. You are looking at a field concerned with the interactions between computers and human languages and programming computers to manipulate large sets of languages. What is the field called?

A. Boltzmann Machine.

B. PCA.

C. Latent Dirichlet Allocation.

D. NLP.

63. What is an EM Algorithm?

A. An iterative method to determine MLE or MOM for models that depend on unobserved latent variable, which uses two steps, the O Step and the M Step, to do so.

B. A non-parametric method of estimating the probability density function of a random variable, where a finite data sample is used to make inferences about the population.

C. Used for inference in graphical models with cyclic structures, or for implementing Bayesian methods that use distribution on parameters.

D. An iterative method to determine MLE or MAP for models that depend on unobserved latent variable, which uses two steps, the E Step and the M Step, to do so.

64. Which of the following best describes Additive Logistic Regression?

    A. Method that, if base learner reduces squared error, can minimize squared error for the ensemble, and perform automatic attribute selection, and prevent overfitting.
    B. A boosting algorithm that maximizes probability when base learner minimizes squared error, which can be used in multi-class problems and avoiding overfitting.
    C. Algorithm for class probability estimation, which can get an algorithm for classification by using additive regression alongside logit transformation.
    D. A type of regularization used while training a learner with an iterative method, in order to prevent overfitting.

65. Which iterative optimization algorithm goes with the negative of the gradient, to find the local minimum of a function?

    A. Gradient Boosting.
    B. Gradient Descent.
    C. Stochastic Learning.
    D. Gradient Ascent.

66. You are looking at a boosting algorithm that maximizes probability when base learner minimizes squared error, which can be used in multi-class problems. What is the algorithm called?

    A. Additive Logistic Regression.
    B. Additive Regression.
    C. Early Stopping.
    D. LogitBoost.

67. What is a statistical Markov model where the system in context is assumed to be a Markov process with hidden or unobserved states, called?

    A. SVM Model.
    B. Mixture Model.
    C. Hidden Markov Model.
    D. Hidden Variable Model.

68. You are looking at an open-source deep learning toolkit developed by Microsoft Research, which describes neural networks as a series of computational steps. What is the toolkit called?

    A. RoomAlive.
    B. WinMine.
    C. CNTK.
    D. Microsoft Research Storage Toolkit.

69. Which of the following can be considered as a relevant way of implementing deep learning in Weka?

    A. Using the wrapper classifiers available in the third-party DeepLearning4J package.

B. Using the multi-layer perceptron classifiers available in the third-party Caffe package.

C. Exploiting deep learning implementations for R with the use of RBFClassifier from the VIM Plugin Manager.

D. Accessing .Net-based deep learning libraries through the NuGet package.

70. You are looking at a concept that is used for inference in graphical models with cyclic structures, or for implementing Bayesian methods. What is the concept called?

A. Probabilistic Inference.

B. Sampling.

C. Hyperparameter Tuning

D. Data Augmentation.

71. What is Long Short Term Memory?

A. A type of neural network where the hidden units are not random variables, hence the connections between the units do not form a cycle.

B. A type of stochastic Markov random field, used usually for unsupervised learning, where units correspond to random variables.

C. A stochastic neural network that learns a probability distribution over a set of inputs, only with the restriction that its neurons should form a bipartite graph.

D. An RNN that uses a combination of hidden units and remembers values over arbitrary intervals, which tackles the vanishing gradient problem.

72. What is the technique in NLP that analyzes relationships between a set of documents and their terms, by creating a set of concepts related to the documents and terms, called?

A. Latent Semantic Analysis.

B. Latent Dirichlet Allocation.

C. Principal Component Analysis.

D. Boltzmann Allocation.

73. Which of the following best describes the capabilities of Neural Networks?

A. Used for image analysis as it is capable of learning both the classifier, and the filter using backpropagation and SGD.

B. Function of a node that determines the output of that specific node, given an input or a set of inputs.

C. Used for unsupervised learning, that is capable of learning efficient coding by learning representation of a data set for dimensionality reduction.

D. Capable of learning to do new tasks, and progressively improving performance, by looking at examples, and without being specifically programmed.

74. What is the method called that, if base learner reduces squared error, can minimize squared error for the ensemble, and perform automatic attribute selection, and prevent overfitting?

   A. Additive Regression.
   B. Early Stopping.
   C. LogitBoost.
   D. Additive Logistic Regression.

75. Which of the following best describes Decision Trees?

   A. Trees with option nodes where predictions from different branches are merged either by averaging probability estimates or by voting.
   B. An ensemble learning meta-algorithm that uses intuitive justification and an iterative model to reduce bias and variance in supervised learning.
   C. Predictive machine learning method that adopts a transparent way of classifying observations, and sequencing what look like a set of if-then statements, into a tree.
   D. Method that, if base learner reduces squared error, can minimize squared error for the ensemble, and perform automatic attribute selection, and prevent overfitting.

76. You want to know more about the ways of implementation in deep learning in Weka. Which of the following can be considered as a relevant way?

   A. Accessing Python-based deep learning libraries through the PyScript package.
   B. Exploiting deep learning implementations for R with the use of RBFClassifier from the VIM Plugin Manager.
   C. Using the multi-layer perceptron classifiers available in the third-party Caffe package.
   D. Accessing .Net-based deep learning libraries through the NuGet package.

77. What is a Factor Graph?

   A. Directed and usually acyclic graphs that help keep track of how complicated computations decompose.
   B. A process of using a specific value, or set of values, and deriving the probability of one or more random variables.
   C. A probabilistic graphical model which is an undirected graph that is associated with a subset of variables and has a non-empty intersection.
   D. A probabilistic graphical model with two types of nodes, variable nodes and factor nodes, for each function, with edges connecting factor nodes to their variables.

71

78. What is Restricted Boltzmann Machine (RBM)?

    A. A stochastic neural network that learns a probability distribution over a set of inputs, only with the restriction that its neurons should form a bipartite graph.
    B. A type of stochastic Markov random field, used usually for unsupervised learning, where units correspond to random variables.
    C. Meta-algorithm that improves the accuracy and stability of machine learning algorithms by combining predictions through methods of averaging or voting.
    D. A type of binary pairwise Markov random field involving coupling layers of hidden random variables, using RBM connectivity.

79. What is the method of using optimization algorithms to select values that minimize the output of a cost function, called?

    A. Gradient Descent.
    B. Optimization.
    C. Simulated Annealing.
    D. Random Searching.

80. What is a type of neural network called, where the hidden units are not random variables, hence the connections between the units do not form a cycle?

    A. Recurrent Neural Networks.
    B. Deep Feedforward Networks.
    C. Deep Belief Network.
    D. Convolutional Neural Networks (CNN).

81. What is the statistical model of representing probability distributions in a graphical way, drawn out as a network of nodes connected by directed edges, as an acyclic graph, called?

    A. Bayesian Networks.
    B. Latent Dirichlet Allocation.
    C. Hidden Markov Model.
    D. Hidden Variable Model.

82. Which of the following can be best described as Recommender Systems?

    A. Set of data used to evaluate the strength and usability of a predictive relationship.
    B. Subclass of a filtering system that aims at predicting a user's preference to a given item.
    C. Set of data used to find possible predictive relationships.
    D. Set of data having numerical features, with n-dimension, representing objects and enabling statistical analysis.

83. What is a Markov Chain?

    A. A statistical Markov model where the system in context is assumed to be a Markov process with hidden or unobserved states.

B. A statistical Markov process of using a specific value, or set of values, and deriving the probability of one or more random variables.

C. A Markov process of increasing the number of data points, and in turn the data size to be fed to machine learning classifiers, that saves cost and time in data collection.

D. A Markov process that has either discrete index set, or discrete state space, usually representing time.

84. Which of the following best describes Test Set?

A. Set of data used to evaluate the strength and usability of a predictive relationship.

B. Subclass of a filtering system that aims at predicting a user's preference to a given item.

C. Set of data having numerical features, with n-dimension, representing objects and enabling statistical analysis.

D. Set of data used to find possible predictive relationships.

85. You are looking at a machine learning method based on learning data representation, instead of the traditional task-specific algorithms. What is the method called?

A. Early Stopping.

B. Deep Learning.

C. Data Augmentation.

D. Hyperparameter Tuning.

86. You are looking at an open-source script language based on the Lua programming language, that offers several algorithms for deep learning. What is the concept called?

A. Caffe.

B. Lasagne.

C. Torch.

D. Deeplearning4j.

8
Bioinformatics

1. What is the method that uses background correction, normalization, and summarization to preprocess probe intensities and make biologically relevant conclusions possible, called?

   A. Gene Filtering.
   B. Mismatch (MM) Probes.
   C. Robust Multiarray Analysis (RMA).
   D. Micro-Array Preprocessing.

2. When GO numbers are found by using the get function to extract a list from annotation files, and to select them with evidence, the subset function is used. What is the concept called?

   A. Searching GO Numbers and Evidence.
   B. Searching an OBO (Open Biomedical Ontology).
   C. Searching an Annotation Package.
   D. Annotating GO Numbers and classifying.

3. What is the process of testing if genes with significant p-values in a t-test, occur more often within a certain chromosome, called?

   A. Significance per Annotation function.
   B. Micro-Array Preprocessing.
   C. Gene Filtering by a Biological Term.
   D. Significance per Chromosome.

4. Which of the following can be considered as a Step for Gene Filtering by a Biological Term?

   A. Use z-function to find the ontology package used in the data collection stage.
   B. Define a function to collect appropriate GO numbers.
   C. Combine the paired t-test to be used with the previous filter.
   D. Using GO numbers and children identifiers, search for probes of the said term.

5. You want to find out ways of Applying Linear Models to Micro-Array Data. Which of the following is the most relevant way?

   A. By the relative standard deviation (RSD).
   B. Using z-test and normality.
   C. By using ANOVA.
   D. By smoothening data with approximating function.

6. What is Searching an Annotation Package?

   A. GO numbers can be found by using set function to modify a list from robust files, to combine them with evidence, the z-test can be used.
   B. The put function can be used to search for an identifier in an environment once the subset of the environment is modified into a list and part of it filtered and displayed on the screen.
   C. The get function can be used to search for a name in an environment once the content of the environment is converted into a list and part of it printed on the screen.
   D. GO numbers can be found by using get function to extract a list from annotation files, to select them with evidence, the subset function can be used.

7. Which of the following can be considered as a way to Obtain GO Parents and Children Identifiers?

   A. Probe Selection: Use annotation function to find the annotation package used in the data collection stage.
   B. Vector: If you have a list of GO identifiers, you can collect the ontology, parents, and children identifiers in a vector.
   C. Probe Selection: Start with filters, find ontology functions, obtain p-values, and transform them into probes.
   D. Vector: Define a function to collect appropriate GO numbers, and identifiers in a vector.

8. You are looking at Ways to Obtain GO Parents and Children Identifiers. Which of the following can be considered as a relevant way?

   A. Probe Selection: Start with filters, find ontology functions, obtain p-values, and transform them into probes.
   B. Probe Selection: Start with probe number, find GO identifiers, obtain its parents, and transform them into probes.
   C. Vector: Define a function to collect appropriate GO numbers, and identifiers in a vector.
   D. Probe Selection: Use annotation function to find the annotation package used in the data collection stage.

9. What is Probe Data?

A. Raw data obtained by measuring the intensity of hybridization of probe to the target molecule.

B. Basic tool for metallurgical research, where all atoms must be analyzed to establish physical parameters and compared to determine limits of confidence.

C. Advanced microanalysis technique that blends position-sensitive ion detection with time and flight mass spectroscopy.

D. Method that uses the tessellation of solute molecules to test for spatial randomness of the solid solution while extracting clusters.

10. You want to know more about Steps for Gene Filtering by a Biological Term. Which of the following can be considered as a relevant step?

A. Using GO numbers and children identifiers, search for probes of the said term.

B. Define a filter to collect appropriate t-test values.

C. Combine the term to be used with the previous filter.

D. Use z-function to find the ontology package used in the data collection stage.

11. Which of the following is a relevant Gene Filtering Method?

A. By smoothening data with approximating function.

B. By the relative standard deviation (RSD).

C. Using z-test and normality.

D. By combining many filters.

77

Python and Libraries

1. Which open-source library of machine learning algorithms is written in Java, for data mining tasks like classification, regression, etc.?

    A. Gensim.
    B. Weka.
    C. Pandas.
    D. Theano.

2. Which of the following best describes Matplotlib?

    A. A high-level plotting library for Python to create graphs, in a variety of formats like eps, png, jpeg, xpm, and also scatter plots.
    B. A graphing library that makes interactive and publication-quality graphs including 3D (WebGL based) charts.
    C. A plotting library for Python that generates high quality and highly customizable graphs, using aggregator daemon and API tools.
    D. A 2D plotting library for Python and NumPy, that offers an object-oriented API for embedding plots into applications.

3. What is Python?

    A. Open-source software framework based on Java, that is ideal for distributed storage and handling of very large amounts of data.
    B. Highly extensible programming language that offers a many graphical and statistical techniques, used primarily in data analysis and statistical software.
    C. An object-oriented, interpreted, high-level programming language that offers code readability, and constructs for writing large and small scale programs clearly.
    D. Applied field in Artificial Intelligence that focuses on training computer programs with algorithms

that allow them to learn without being specifically programmed.

4. The occurrence when two different keys are hashed to the same slot, or have the same hash code, is called as:

   A. HashMap Collision.
   B. Hash Table Collision.
   C. Knapsack Problem.
   D. Separate Chaining.

5. What is TensorFlow?

   A. A neural networks library for Python that provides flexible yet high-performance algorithms for machine learning tasks, and environments to test and compare them.
   B. Library for machine learning, that uses data flow graphs to create and train neural networks to identify and analyze patterns analogous to human learning and reasoning.
   C. Open-source numerical computation library for Python that enables efficient defining and optimizing of mathematical expressions that involve multi-dimensional arrays.
   D. A data analysis library for Python, that provides flexible and fast data structures and operations for manipulating time series and numerical tables.

6. What is an open-source topic modeling and vector space modeling toolkit for Python, designed to deal with large text collections, called?

   A. Pandas.
   B. Gensim.
   C. Matplotlib.
   D. Theano.

7. Which of the following best describes PyBrain?

   A. Open-source numerical computation library for Python that enables efficient defining and optimizing of mathematical expressions that involve multi-dimensional arrays.
   B. Library for machine learning, that uses data flow graphs to create and train neural networks to identify and analyze patterns analogous to human learning and reasoning.
   C. A neural networks library for Python that provides flexible yet high-performance algorithms for machine learning tasks, and environments to test and compare them.
   D. A data analysis library for Python, that provides flexible and fast data structures and operations for manipulating time series and numerical tables.

8. Which of the following best describes Python MySQL?

   A. A MySQL Pure Scala client interface that enables connectivity to a MySQL server from operating systems on which MySQL is ported.

B. A MySQL Pure Perl client interface that enables connectivity to a MySQL server from operating systems on which MySQL is not ported.

C. Enables Python programs to access MySQL databases, using an API that is compliant with the Python Database API Specification v2.0 (PEP 249).

D. Enables Python programs to access any database, using JDBC that is compliant with the Python Database API Specification v4.0 (PEP 279).

9. You are looking at a problem where, a set of items with a value and a weight are chosen to fit a maximum weight limit, while keeping the total value high. What is the problem called?

   A. Traveling Salesman Problem.
   B. Knapsack Problem.
   C. Subset Sum Problem.
   D. Cutting Stock Problem.

10. A platform helps build Python programs for statistical and symbolic natural language processing for English written in Python. What is the platform called?

    A. NLTK.
    B. TensorFlow.
    C. PyBrain.
    D. Weka.

11. What is Theano?

    A. A neural networks library for Python that provides flexible yet high-performance algorithms for machine learning tasks, and environments to test and compare them.

    B. Library for machine learning, that uses data flow graphs to create and train neural networks to identify and analyze patterns analogous to human learning and reasoning.

    C. A data analysis library for Python, that provides flexible and fast data structures and operations for manipulating time series and numerical tables.

    D. Open-source numerical computation library for Python that enables efficient defining and optimizing of mathematical expressions that involve multi-dimensional arrays.

Answers To Statistics

1. The temperature in degrees Celsius over 4 days in Oslo city in October was 12, 15, 14, and 9. What is the mean temperature?
   Answer: C

   12.5

2. What is Multivariate Analysis?
   Answer: B

   Type of statistical analysis than can study complex sets of data like software, etc. by analyzing more than one outcome variable at a time.

3. What is a Bar Graph?
   Answer: C

   Graph that breaks down categorical data into groups, and shows them as rectangular bars, whose lengths and heights are proportional to the values they represent.

4. What is the type of statistical analysis that involves the study of two variables and determines the factual relationship between them, called?
   Answer: C

   Bivariate Analysis.

5. What is a Paired t-test?
   Answer: A

   Similar to the t-test, only, the samples have matched pairs of similar units, or a group of units which is tested twice.

6. What is the Empirical Rule?
   Answer: C

   Rule used to remember the percentage (68.27%, 95.45% and 99.73%) of the values that lie within one, two and three standard deviations of the mean, respectively.

7. What is a Boxplot?
   Answer: A

   One-dimensional graph that depicts groups of numerical data through their quartiles, based on the five-number summary.

8. What is Test Statistic?
   Answer: B

   Statistic that represents the distance between the actual sample results and the claimed population value, in terms of number of standard errors.

9. Which of the following best describes a Pie Chart?
Answer: C

Circular chart that breaks down categorical data into groups, and represents each group as a slice, whose angle and area correspond to its numerical proportion.

10. When the default hypothesis states that the population parameter is equal to the claimed value, and is assumed to be true until proven otherwise, what is it called?
Answer: D

Null Hypothesis (H0).

11. What is Combination?
Answer: C

Total number of ways in which objects can be chosen from a pool, without giving any importance to the order in which they are organized.

12. What is a Histogram?
Answer: A

A type of bar chart which accurately represents the probability distribution of a quantitative variable in graphical manner.

13. Which of the following best describes p-value?
Answer: C

The probability of finding the more extreme, or observed results for a statistical model, when the null hypothesis is true for the study question.

14. Which of the following best describes Multicollinearity?
Answer: C

Multicollinearity occurs when in a multiple regression model, one predictor variable can be linearly predicted from others with significant accuracy.

15. Which of the following is a step in calculating Confidence Interval?
Answer: D

Choose the population statistic.

16. You want to obtain a measure of variation that is based on the five-number summary by finding the interquartile range. What is the interquartile range formula?
Answer: B

IQR = Q3 - Q1. Which means, Interquartile Range is the 1st quartile subtracted from the 3rd quartile.

17. Which of the following best describes Power Analysis?
Answer: D

Used to calculate the minimum sample size required to be fairly likely to find an effect of a given size.

18. Which of the following can be best described as Univariate Analysis?
Answer: B

The simplest type of statistical analysis that describes patterns in data by analyzing only one outcome variable for every observation.

19. Which of the following is a relevant sample percentile in the context of the five-number summary?
Answer: C

The third quartile, or the 75th percentile.

84

20. The temperature in degrees Celsius over 4 days in Prague city in October was 12, 15, 14, and 9. What is the median?
Answer: A

13

21. Which of the following best describes Standard Deviation?
Answer: B

The statistic that reports the relative standing of the mean, median, and SD, indicating the value below which, a given percentage of observations fall.

22. You find that a null hypothesis that is not true, and is not rejected. What is the type of error?
Answer: A

Type 2 Error.

23. Which of the following best describes Standard Deviation?
Answer: A

Standard Deviation (SD) is the value that denotes the variation in numerical data by measuring the concentration of the data around the mean.

24. Which of the following best describes Stacking?
Answer: D

Method of training an algorithm to combine the predictions of multiple models or algorithms as additional inputs to the already available data.

25. Which of the following is a common measure of relative standing?
Answer: A

Quartiles.

26. What is Permutation?
Answer: B

Total number of ways in which a particular number of objects, taken from a bigger group of objects, can be ordered.

27. In the context of a five-number summary, which of the following is a valid sample percentile?
Answer: D

The first quartile, or the 25th percentile of the sample.

28. Which of the following best describes power analysis?
Answer: D

Applied in calculating the minimum effect size, likely to be found in a study with a given sample.

29. Which of the following best describes Margin of Error (MOE)?
Answer: B

The measure of how close the sample statistic is expected to be, to the population parameter being observed.

30. The difference in value for every variable in a given data set, is called as:
Answer: D

Variation.

31. A hypothesis test has one statement that the mean completion time for a survey is 45 minutes, and another statement that the time is > 45 minutes. The second statement is called as:
Answer: A

Alternative Hypothesis (Ha).

32. When a null hypothesis that is true, is rejected, what is the error called?
Answer: B

Type 1 Error.

33. The data that represents characteristics of the observed in numerical values, is called as:
Answer: D

Categorical Data.

34. What is the standard deviation of a statistic's (usually the mean) sampling distribution, or in some cases, an estimate of such a standard deviation, called?
Answer: B

Standard Error (SE).

35. A type of chart that is used to display trends in data over a time period (x-axis) where data is denoted as a series of points or markers joined by straight lines (y-axis) is called as:
Answer: B

Time Chart/Line Graph.

36. What is the concept called, for the statistic that divides an ordered distribution into four parts, which are the quarters of the population?
Answer: A

Quartiles.

37. When a value measures the proportion of positives which are accurately identified, e.g. percentage of sick people correctly identified as having the condition, what is it called?
Answer: B

Sensitivity.

38. What is the concept called, for a type of interval estimate computed from the observed data of a population parameter?
Answer: C

Confidence Interval.

39. Analysis of two population means where the test statistic follows a t-distribution under the null hypothesis, is called as:
Answer: A

t-test.

40. In the context of the five-number summary, which of the following is a relevant sample percentile?
Answer: B

The sample minimum, which is the smallest observation.

41. What is Interquartile Range?
Answer: D

A measure of statistical dispersion that shows the distance taken up by the innermost 50% of the data, derived at, by subtracting Q1 from Q3.

42. You are exploring a probabilistic technique that offers a mechanism to make quantitative decisions and has enough evidence to reject or accept a conjecture. What is the technique called?
Answer: B

Statistical Hypothesis.

11

Answers To Linear Models and Regression

1. How is a Continuous Random Variable defined?
   Answer: B

   Random variables that usually represent measurements, and whose possible outcomes can be described only using an interval of real numbers.

2. When a model cannot capture the underlying trend in the data, resulting in inadequate predictive performance, what is the concept called?
   Answer: C

   Underfitting.

3. Which of the following can be considered as a condition for a Binomial Distribution?
   Answer: B

   Is the number of trials fixed?

4. You are looking at a regression technique that is used primarily for numeric prediction, that expresses the class as a linear combination of the attributes. What is the technique called?
   Answer: A

   Linear Regression.

5. You want to know more about the Generalized Linear Model (GLM). Which of the following best describes GLM?
   Answer: D

   A generalization of linear regression that is flexible, and allows for response variables that have other kind of error distribution models than a normal distribution.

6. What is a Linear model?
   Answer: A

   A type of regression model where significant reduction in the complexity of the related statistical theory is attainable.

7. Which of the following best describes the General Linear Model?
   Answer: B

   Written as Y=XB+U, this is a statistical linear model.

8. Which of the following best describes the traveling salesman problem?
   Answer: D

   A nondeterministic polynomial-time-hard problem in combinatorial optimization, significant in the fields of theoretical computer science and operations research.

9. What is the method of adding more data as a countermeasure against overfitting, or to tackle an ill-posed problem, called?
Answer: B

Regularization.

10. What is Matrix transpose?
Answer: B

Operator that creates another matrix by switching the row and column indices of the matrix, which means flipping the matrix over its diagonal.

11. What is the random variable that usually represent counts, and whose possible outcomes can be listed using whole numbers, called?
Answer: D

Discrete Random Variable.

12. What is Gamma Distribution?
Answer: A

A type of general distribution which is a two-parameter family of continuous probability distributions, alpha and theta being the two free parameters.

13. Which of the following best describes t-distribution?
Answer: A

A family of distributions identical to the normal distribution, but used when the sample size is much smaller, and the population SD is unknown.

14. What is Normality Assumption?
Answer: B

Normality assumptions can be tested as a null hypothesis, using the Shapiro-Wilk test.

15. You want to know more about the conditions for a Binomial Distribution. Which of the following is a valid condition?
Answer: A

Are the trials independent?

16. The inverse of a square matrix, which, in case the invertible matrix is A, is denoted as A to the power minus one, is called as:
Answer: C

Matrix inverse.

17. Which of the following best describes Poisson Distribution?
Answer: C

A discrete probability distribution that is valid only if the events happen independently of the time since the last event, and with a known constant.

18. Which of the following is a relevant parameter that defines Normal Distribution?
Answer: D

The Mu, which refers to the center of the curve.

19. What is a Random Variable?
Answer: B

A variable, measurement, or characteristic that changes randomly as per a pattern, and whose possible values are numerical outcomes of a random occurrence.

20. What is the distribution for continuous data called, in a symmetrical bell curve, with the center of the curve representing the highest probability density?
Answer: D

Normal Distribution.

21. You are looking at a regression technique that creates a linear model based on a transformed target variable where the dependent variable is categorical. What is the concept called?
Answer: A

Logistic Regression.

22. What is the continuous probability distribution of a random variable with a normally distributed logarithm, called?
Answer: C

Lognormal Distribution.

23. You want to know more about the Probability Density of the Bell Curve in a Normal Distribution. Which of the following is the most relevant in the context?
Answer: C

Both the mean and the median are at the center, and have the highest probability density, and so, as you move away from this center, the density decreases.

24. What is Overfitting?
Answer: C

Occurs when the performance of a model on new data is negatively affected because of the model being too complex, and picking up even the noise in the training data.

25. Which of the following best describes Probability Distribution?
Answer: B

A function showing all the probabilities of all possible values of a discrete random variable, occurring in an experiment.

26. You want to know about a type of variance analysis that is used to check if there are statistically significant differences between 3 or more population means. What is the concept called?
Answer: A

One-way Analysis of Variance.

27. Which of the following best describes Homoscedasticity assumption?
Answer: A

Homoscedasticity assumptions can be tested as a hypothesis, using the Breusch and Pagan test.

28. What is Binomial Distribution?
Answer: A

The discrete probability distribution of the number of successes in a sequence of 'n' independent experiments, each asking a yes-no question.

29. You are looking for a statistical technique that is used to find percentiles for regular normal distributions having a mean of zero and a SD of 1. What is the technique called?
Answer: D

z-distribution.

30. You want to know more about Bernoulli Distribution. Which of the following best describes the concept?
Answer: A

A discrete binomial distribution where a single trial is conducted, which has two possible outcomes, success (n=1), and failure (n=0).

31. You want to know more about Robust Test. Which of the following best describes the concept?
Answer: C

89

Alternative assumption testing method used when normality or homoscedasticity assumptions produce results with unequal variances.

32. What is Sampling Distribution?
Answer: B

Probability distribution of a given statistic, based on a random sample that hugely simplify the ways to reach statistical inference.

33. What is the standard deviation of a statistic's (usually the mean) sampling distribution, or in some cases, an estimate of such a standard deviation, called?
Answer: B

Standard Error (SE).

34. What is a Two-way Analysis of Variance?
Answer: C

Type of variance analysis used to compare the differences in mean between groups that are split on two factors or independent variables.

35. What is the statistical process that determines the strength of the relationship between one fixed dependent variable, and a series of changing independent variables called?
Answer: C

Regression.

36. Which of the following can be best described as the General Linear Model?
Answer: C

Y=XB+U, where: Y is a matrix with series of multivariate measurements; X is a design matrix; B is a matrix of parameters to be estimated; and U is a matrix of noise.

37. When a discrete probability distribution asserts the probability of a given number of events happening in a fixed interval of time and/or space, what is the distribution called?
Answer: C

Poisson Distribution.

12

Answers To Relational Algebra

1. Which of the following can be best described as the Rename operation in Relational Algebra?
   Answer: D

   A unary operation that lets you assign a name to the results of a relational-algebra expression.

2. What is the binary operation that can create an implicit join clause based on common columns in the two tables that are being joined, called?
   Answer: A

   Natural Join.

3. What is a family of algebras used for defining queries on relational databases, and modeling the data stored in them, giving a theoretical foundation, called?
   Answer: A

   Relational Algebra.

4. What is the Union operation in Relational Algebra?
   Answer: A

   A binary operation that returns the results that appear in one or both of the two relations.

5. Which of the following can be considered as Fundamental operations in Relational Algebra?
   Answer: C

   Select.

6. What is an operation that assigns expressions to a temporary relation variable?
   Answer: D

   Assignment.

7. What is the Select operation in Relational Algebra?
   Answer: D

   A unary operation that selects tuples that satisfy a specific predicate.

8. You want to know more about a unary operation that returns its argument relation with a few attributes excluded. What is the operation called?
   Answer: C

   Project.

9. Which of the following best describes Set-intersection?
   Answer: C

Operation that yields the tuples that are present in both relations the operation is applying to.

10. What is the operation that yields tuples that are present in one relation and not in another, called?
Answer: A

Set difference.

11. You want to know more about an operation that can combine information from two relations. What is the operation called?
Answer: D

Cartesian Product.

12. What is the Division operation in Relational Algebra?
Answer: B

Division.

13

Answers To SQL

1. Which of the following best describes the Update Row command?
   Answer: B

   Statement used to change the data in a row of a table. You can choose to update all the rows at once, or, choose a subset with the use of a condition.

2. What is the Time data type?
   Answer: A

   A data type that can store a point in time, including hours, minutes, seconds and usually, milliseconds.

3. What are ACID properties?
   Answer: D

   Properties of database transactions that aim at guaranteeing validity despite events of power failures, errors, etc.

4. Which of the following best describes Relational Algebra?
   Answer: C

   A family of algebras used for defining queries on relational databases, and modeling the data stored in them, giving a theoretical foundation.

5. What are Ordered Indices?
   Answer: D

   A type of lookup table that can be created for each column that is important, in order to optimize the performance of SQL databases.

6. Which of the following best describes Replication?
   Answer: A

   Process of synchronizing databases with each other based on specific criteria set by the programmer, in order to securely backup data and avoid data loss.

7. When a stored procedure executes commonly required actions automatically during a specific event occurring in the database server, what is this called?
   Answer: C

   Trigger.

8. Which of the following best describes an RDBMS?
   Answer: A

   Database management system designed by Edgar F. Codd of IBM, which is based on the relational model.

93

9. Which of the following best describes 1NF?
Answer: D

Property of a relation in a relational database, where first normal is a minimum requirement, and each column type is unique, with no group/type of data repeated.

10. When the property of a relation in a relational database minimizes data duplication by ensuring that no entry in a table is dependent on any other entry except the key. What is the NF?
Answer: B

3NF.

11. What is the String data type?
Answer: A

A sequence of characters that can either be any kind of variable, or a literal constant.

12. What is a non-relational and largely distributed database environment that allows for high-speed, ad-hoc analysis and organizing of high-volume data types called?
Answer: D

NoSQL.

13. When a clause is used on multiple tables to return a result as one table, based on a related column between the tables, what is this called?
Answer: A

Join.

14. When sets of rules used are applied during the creation of a database, for the purposes of database normalization, what is the concept called?
Answer: A

Forms.

15. What is a Foreign Key?
Answer: C

Field in a database table that refers to the primary key in another table.

16. Which of the following best describes Left Join?
Answer: B

Operation that returns all the records from the table on the left, and only the matched records from the table on the right.

17. When storage devices are located at various locations of a network, without being attached to a common processor, what is the database type called?
Answer: A

Distributed Databases (DDB).

18. How is a Table defined?
Answer: B

Set of data values in a relational database in the form of rows and columns, where a cell is the point of intersection between a row and a column.

19. What is the query command in SQL that allows you to assign the result of a query to a new private table?
Answer: C

View.

20. What is an Outer Join?
Answer: C

Operation where the resulting table retains all the rows even if there are no matching rows.

21. What is a mechanism in RDBMS that protects the data integrity during server failures or when multiple users try to access the data at the same time?
Answer: C

Transaction.

22. How is Drop Table defined?
Answer: A

Statement used to delete a table definition, and all corresponding details including all the data, permission specifications, constraints, triggers, and indexes.

23. A property that decides how transaction integrity is visible to other users, while ensuring that processes don't interfere with others. What is it called?
Answer: B

Integrity.

24. Which element allows users to decide how data is stored in a database, and how it is used?
Answer: B

Data Type.

25. Which of the following best describes Right Join?
Answer: C

Operation that returns all the records from the table on the right, and only the matched records from the table on the left.

26. What is clustering?
Answer: A

Simplest way of optimizing an SQL database, where the contents of the database are organized in the same way as data is requested frequently.

27. Which of the following can be considered as a basic command in SQL?
Answer: D

INSERT - for inserting data.

28. What is the collection of data, in the form of tables, schemas, reports, queries, etc., arranged in a specific way, called?
Answer: A

Database.

29. When a statement is used to insert a new row to an existing table in a database, what is the sequel command?
Answer: D

Insert Row.

30. You are looking at database normalization where a normal form involves keeping all attributes within an entity depending solely on the unique identifier of the entity. What is the NF?
Answer: B

2NF.

31. What is SQL?
Answer: B

Domain-specific language used primarily to manage data in a relational database management system, which uses a single command to access many records.

32. Which of the following can be considered as a defining characteristic of a Procedural language?
Answer: D

File-oriented.

33. You are looking at the DBMS that supports modeling of data as objects, by integrating database capabilities with the capabilities

95

of object-oriented programming languages. What is the DBMS called?
Answer: B

ODBMS.

34. Which of the following best describes a Row?
Answer: D

Field representing a single, implicitly structured data item in a table.

35. When the normal form separates semantically related multiple relationships, minimizes redundancies in relational databases that record multivalued facts, what is the NF?
Answer: B

5NF.

36. Which of the following best describes procedures?
Answer: B

Subroutines that are written only once and stored in the database data dictionary, and are available to any programming language that interacts with the database.

37. In the admission database, you want to add a new student table. What SQL statement is relevant in the context?
Answer: A

CREATE TABLE student;

38. What is the Fourth Normal Form (4NF)?
Answer: D

Normal form used in database normalization, which, unlike other normal forms that are concerned with functional dependencies, is concerned with multivalued dependency.

39. Which of the following best describes the integer data type?
Answer: B

A data type that represents some finite subset of the mathematical integers.

40. Which of the following best describes the Consistency element in ACID properties?
Answer: A

Property that requires a transaction to change affected data only in specifically allowed ways.

41. What is the API used for DBMS access that is independent of operating systems and/or database systems called?
Answer: B

ODBC.

42. You have added a row in the student table in the admission database, but you wish to delete the row. Which of the following SQL command is relevant?
Answer: C

Delete Row is a statement used to delete a row in an existing table in a database.

43. When a property of a set of irreducible and indivisible set of database operations are considered as one operation, where either nothing occurs, or all occur, what is the property called?
Answer: D

Atomicity.

44. What is JDBC?
Answer: C

API used for Java database connectivity, that determines how a client using a Java run application can access the database.

45. When a data type can store a value such as 01/01/2019, what is the data type?
Answer: D

Date.

46. Which of the following best describes an inner join?
Answer: C

Operation that returns only the records that have matching column values in both the tables.

47. The maximum temperature in October in Toronto was 13.4 degree Celsius. Which data type would be the best to store the value?
Answer: C

Float.

48. What is the Durability property?
Answer: D

Property that ensures that changes caused by a transaction survive permanently.

49. You want to store a set of binary data as a single entity, primarily in the form of multimedia objects like audio or images. What datatype should be used?
Answer: D

Blob.

14

Answers To NoSQL

1. Which of the following can be considered as a General Type of NoSQL Database?
   Answer: B

   Document Database.

2. Which of the following best describes a Cursor?
   Answer: D

   Pointer to the results of a query that is returned for any query run, where clients can iterate through the cursor to retrieve documents.

3. Which of the following best describes Integrated Caching?
   Answer: D

   Feature of NoSQL databases that minimize the need for separate caching layers by storing frequently-used data in system memory to the maximum extent possible.

4. You want a Python distribution that offers tools to work with MongoDB, which is also a suggested distribution to work with MongoDB from Python. What is the distribution called?
   Answer: D

   PyMongo.

5. What is the feature that allows insertion of data into NoSQL databases without a predefined schema, enabling faster coding, more reliable code integration, and less admin time, called?
   Answer: D

   Dynamic Schema.

6. In NoSQL databases, data on one node could become out of sync with another node. What is this property called?
   Answer: B

   Data Consistency.

7. What is the name-value pair in a MongoDB document, which is much like a column in a relational DB, called?
   Answer: B

   Field.

8. Which of the following database transaction properties is provided by a BASE system?
   Answer: A

   Soft-state.

9. Which of the following best describes Real Location Independence?
Answer: C

NoSQL allows read and write operations, irrespective of where the operation occurs physically, making the database available to users at multiple locations.

10. What is a non-relational and largely distributed database environment that allows for high-speed, ad-hoc analysis and organizing of high-volume data types?
Answer: D

NoSQL.

11. You are looking at a data storage and network transfer format used in MongoDB, which is a binary variant for representing MongoDB documents in different data types. What is the format called?
Answer: D

BSON.

12. What is the mandatory field for every MongoDB document that represents a unique value, and acts as the primary key of the document called?
Answer: B

_id.

13. Which of the following best describes Riak?
Answer: B

A distributed NoSQL key-value data store that fault-tolerant, highly available, and easily scalable.

14. What is DynamoDB?
Answer: C

A proprietary, NoSQL database service that offers high availability, scalability, and durability, and uses synchronous replication across various data centers.

15. When an open-source, in-memory database management system supports many abstract data structures like strings, hyperlog logs, etc., and offers durability, what is the system called?
Answer: A

Redis.

16. When the most recent write, or an error, for every read is guaranteed, and all servers have the same data to ensure uniform query results, what is the concept called?
Answer: A

Replication.

17. You are looking at a data storage that has an undetermined number of relations, all of which are represented as a graph, with interconnected elements. What type of NoSQL database is this?
Answer: B

Graph Database.

18. You are looking at an open-source, NoSQL, cross-platform database that is document oriented, and uses documents similar to JSON with schemas. What is the database called?
Answer: D

MongoDB.

19. What is a Collection?
Answer: A

The grouping of documents in MongoDB, like tables in other RDBMS services, which don't require any kind of structure.

20. What is Replication?
    Answer: C

    Feature of NoSQL databases that provide automatic replication of data in order to maintain availability during maintenance events or outages.

21. What is the feature that spreads data across multiple servers, automatically balancing data and query load across servers, and replacing servers without application disruption, called?
    Answer: C

    Auto-sharding.

22. What is a Document?
    Answer: C

    Individual records saved in a MongoDB collection, which store data in the form of field names and values.

23. Which of the following best describes Giraph?
    Answer: B

    An iterative database system designed for high scalability and graph processing on big data that uses Hadoop MapReduce implementation.

24. Which of the following best describes Lack of Standardization in NoSQL?
    Answer: C

    As NoSQL does not support a standard query language, it could cause issues during migration of databases from other environments.

25. Which of the following best describes Partition Tolerance?
    Answer: C

    Guarantees continuous operation of the system as a whole, regardless of any messages being delayed or dropped between nodes, or any failure of individual servers.

26. When each key is paired with a document, which is nothing but a complex data structure that may have several key-value pairs, or nested documents, what is the concept called?
    Answer: A

    Document Databases.

27. What is Continuous Data Availability?
    Answer: D

    In NoSQL databases, if one or more servers or nodes go down, other servers and nodes can continue operating without any loss of data.

28. You are looking at a container in which collections are stored on MongoDB, with its own set of files on the file system. What is the concept called?
    Answer: D

    Database.

29. What is Hbase?
    Answer: B

    An open-source, NoSQL, distributed, column-oriented database built on HDFS, that offers horizontal scaling and random real-time read/write access to data on Hadoop.

30. You are looking at a distributed data store that can only provide two of these three guarantees at a time: Consistency, Availability, and Partition Tolerance. What is

101

the concept called?
Answer: B

CAP Theorem.

31. You are looking at an open-source, NoSQL, distributed database that handles large data sets across many commodity servers with no single point of failure. What is the database called?
Answer: B

Cassandra.

32. Which of the following best describes JavaScript Object Notation?
Answer: A

Data format for expressing structured data in a plain text, human readable form, and is supported in several programming languages.

33. What is Availability?
Answer: B

Guarantees a non-error response to every request, whether or not it includes the most recent write.

34. You want to know more about the elements to be considered before choosing a NoSQL database. Which of the following is a relevant element most specific to NoSQL?
Answer: B

Scalability.

35. What is Neo4J?
Answer: C

An open-source, NoSQL, ACID-compliant graph database management system, that provides native graph storage and processing.

36. When data tables are stored together, as sections of columns of data, instead of rows, providing a high performing scalable design for large datasets, what is the concept called?
Answer: D

Wide column stores.

37. What is a Flexible Data Model?
Answer: D

NoSQL databases can house all types of data, even those without a schema like structured, semi-structured, and unstructured data.

38. Which of the following is an element to be considered before choosing a NoSQL database?
Answer: A

Performance.

39. You are looking at an open-source, NoSQL, document-oriented database software that uses JSON for data storage, and aims at providing scalability. What is the database called?
Answer: D

CouchDB.

40. Which of the following best describes Berkeley DB?
Answer: D

An open-source, NoSQL, embedded software library that supports multiple data items for a single key, and offers a high-performance, scalable, database.

41. What is a Key Value store?
Answer: D

Store data in a schema-less manner, where each item is stored along with its value, in the form of an indexed key (or an attribute name).

15

Answers To Hadoop

1. Built on Hadoop YARN, which extesible framework enables building of high-performance data processing applications?
   Answer: C

   Apache Tez.

2. Which software platform that runs on Apache Hadoop, helps build programs, and executes Hadoop jobs?
   Answer: C

   Apache Pig.

3. Which of the following best describes Apache Hive?
   Answer: A

   A data warehouse software built on Hadoop, that offers data summarization, query, and analysis for large data sets, and uses SQL as it's query language.

4. What is Hadoop?
   Answer: D

   Open-source software framework based on Java, that is ideal for distributed storage and handling of very large amounts of data.

5. Which of the following best describes Apache Zookeeper?
   Answer: C

   A cross-platform service that offers a key-value store for distributed configuration, synchronization, and naming registry services for large systems.

6. What is Apache Ambari?
   Answer: B

   Open-source distributed computing platform for provisioning, managing, and monitoring Hadoop clusters, and integrating existing enterprise infrastructure with Hadoop.

7. What is an open-source framework for cluster-computing that offers an interface for programming entire clusters with fault-tolerance, and implicit data-parallelism, called?
   Answer: B

   Apache Spark.

8. What is the Library of distributed machine-learning algorithms in areas of classification, clustering,

and collaborative filtering, implemented using MapReduce, on Hadoop, called?
Answer: A

Apache Mahout.

9. What is the Primary component of the Apache Hadoop framework, which is a programming model used for distributed computing of large amounts of data on a cluster, called?
Answer: B

MapReduce.

10. Which of the following is NOT a common Hadoop input format?
Answer: C

Hash.

11. Which of the following is true in Hadoop, compared to an RDBMS?
Answer: B

Writes are faster.

16

Answers To Machine Learning

1. Which statistical model relates a set of manifest variables to a set of latent variables?
   Answer: A
   Hidden Variable Model.

2. Which of the following can be considered as a weakness of Bayesian classifier?
   Answer: B
   Not equipped to handle outcomes that change due to combinations of features.

3. What is Kernel Density Estimation?
   Answer: B
   A non-parametric method of estimating the probability density function of a random variable, where a finite data sample is used to make inferences about the population.

4. What is the technique that estimates the parameter values that maximize the likelihood of making the observations, for a given statistical model, called?
   Answer: C
   MLE Estimation.

5. Which of the following best describes Supervised Learning?
   Answer: B
   Applications learn to make predictions by first looking at example sets of inputs and outputs, and then applying this learning to a given task.

6. Which of the following can be best described as a Feature Vector?
   Answer: A
   A vector of numerical features, with n-dimension, representing objects and enabling statistical analysis.

7. You are looking at an approach that can turn a linear model into a nonlinear model by replacing its predictors by a kernel function. What is the concept called?
   Answer: C
   The Kernel Trick.

8. Which of the following can be best described as Simulated Annealing?
   Answer: C

Predicts the global optimum of a function by predicting a random solution at first, and improving the same by determining the cost of another random solution.

9. What is a set of data that is used to find possible predictive relationships, called?
Answer: D

Training Set.

10. What is the generative graphical architecture composed of multiple layers of hidden variables where the layers are connected, but not the units between them, called?
Answer: D

Deep Belief Network.

11. Which of the following can be considered as a Common Deep Learning Software Library?
Answer: C

Lasagne.

12. What is Cosine Similarity?
Answer: D

Measure of similarity between 2 non-zero vectors of an inner product space, or two documents on the Vector Space, that computes the cosine of the angle between them.

13. You are looking at directed and acyclic graphs that help keep track of how complicated computations decompose. What is the graph called?
Answer: C

Computation Graphs.

14. Which of the following best describes Caffe?
Answer: B

An open-source deep learning framework written with a Python interface, in C++, primarily supporting image segmentation and image classification.

15. Which of the following best describes Principal Component Analysis?
Answer: D

Procedure that converts observations of possibly correlated variables into values of linearly uncorrelated variables, using an orthogonal transformation.

16. What is Forward Propagation?
Answer: B

Process of multiplying input with weights, and adding bias prior to applying activation function at each node.

17. You are looking at a meta-algorithm that improves the accuracy of machine learning algorithms by combining predictions through methods of averaging. What is the concept called?
Answer: B

Bagging.

18. Which of the following best describes a Boltzmann Machine?
Answer: A

A type of stochastic Markov random field, used usually for unsupervised learning, where units correspond to random variables.

19. What is the technique that on the basis on empirical data, estimates an unknown quantity that equals the mode of the posterior distribution, called?
Answer: C

MAP Estimation.

20. What is the applied field in Artificial Intelligence that focuses on training computer programs with algorithms that allow them to learn without being specifically programmed, called?
Answer: A

Machine Learning.

21. Which of the following best describes Latent Dirichlet Allocation?
Answer: A

Model in NLP for large sets of discrete data like text corpora, which lets sets of observations to be explained for their similarity in data, by unobserved groups.

22. You are looking at autoencoders that can learn low-dimensional representations using the same number of dimensions, with lesser reconstruction error than PCA. What are they called?
Answer: B

Deep Autoencoders.

23. What is the type of binary pairwise Markov random field involving coupling layers of hidden random variables, using RBM connectivity, called?
Answer: D

Deep RBM (Restricted Boltzmann Machine).

24. What is an adjoining sequence of n items from a specified sequence of speech or text, like syllables, base, pairs, phonemes, etc., called?
Answer: C

n-gram.

25. What is the layer in an artificial neural network that converts the inputs into something that can be used by the output layer, called?
Answer: B

Hidden Layer.

26. You are looking at an algorithm that is used for supervised learning of binary classifiers, which processes elements in the training set one at a time. What is the algorithm called?
Answer: B

Perceptron.

27. What is the representation of the set of all hierarchical trees of a specific data set that helps better understanding of hierarchical clusterings, called?
Answer: C

DensiTree.

28. Which of the following best describes Bias-Variance Decomposition?
Answer: C

Method of analyzing an algorithm's expected generalization error as the sum of the bias, variance, and the irreducible error.

29. What is Lasagne?
Answer: D

A lightweight software library that helps build and train neural networks on Theano, which supports feed-forward networks, and offers freely definable cost function.

30. What is the function of a node that determines the output of that specific node, given an input or a set of inputs, called?
Answer: C

Activation Function.

107

31. What is Hyperparameter Tuning?
    Answer: A

    The challenge of selecting a set of optimal hyperparameters for a learning algorithm that maximizes the algorithm's performance.

32. What is MOM Estimation?
    Answer: D

    Technique that estimates population parameters by deriving equations that relate the population moments to the parameters of interest.

33. What are Convolutional Neural Networks (CNN)?
    Answer: C

    A class of deep feedforward neural networks used for image analysis as it is capable of learning both the classifier, and the filter using backpropagation and SGD.

34. You are looking at a function that predicts a solution that is lower for solutions that are better for those that are worse than the one in context. What is the concept called?
    Answer: C

    The Cost Function.

35. What are computing systems that are inspired by the design and functioning of the biological networks in animal brains, called?
    Answer: C

    Neural Networks.

36. What is Naive Bayes?
    Answer: B

    Set of probabilistic classifiers that apply Bayes' theorem with naive independence assumptions between features, and use normal distribution to model numeric attributes.

37. Which of the following best describes Alternating Decision Trees?
    Answer: D

    Type of option tree where nodes are added incrementally using a boosting algorithm, and has splitter nodes and prediction nodes.

38. You are looking at decision trees with option nodes where predictions from different branches are merged by averaging probability estimates or by voting. What is the concept called?
    Answer: C

    Option Trees.

39. What is the clustering algorithm that reduces distance from all points to their cluster centers, and is instructed in advance to generate a specific number of clusters (k), called?
    Answer: B

    k-means.

40. What is Boosting?
    Answer: B

    An ensemble learning meta-algorithm that uses intuitive justification and an iterative model to reduce bias and variance in supervised learning.

41. What is Backpropagation?
    Answer: B

    Algorithm used in artificial neural networks for supervised learning, that calculates the error contribution of each neuron after a data batch is processed.

42. Which of the following can be considered as a Step of EM Algorithm?
Answer: A

E-Step: Calculates the expectations used in the expected log-likelihood.

43. What is cuDNN?
Answer: B

A GPU-accelerated deep neural network library by NVIDIA, designed to offer highly tuned implementations for routines like pooling, convolution, normalization, etc.

44. Which of the following best describes data augmentation?
Answer: C

Process of increasing the number of data points, and in turn the data size to be fed to machine learning classifiers, that saves cost and time in data collection.

45. Which ensemble learning method constructs several decision trees during training, and results in the mean prediction of the classes?
Answer: B

Random Forest.

46. You are looking at a process that uses a specific value, or set of values, and derives the probability of one or more random variables. What is the concept called?
Answer: D

Probabilistic Inference.

47. What is Keras?
Answer: D

An open-source neural network library written in Python, and designed to be minimal, extensible, and modular, and aid fast experimentation with deep neural networks.

48. Which of the following best describes Autoencoders?
Answer: B

A neural network used for unsupervised learning, that is capable of learning efficient coding by learning representation of a data set for dimensionality reduction.

49. When an algorithm is used to generate samples from a joint distribution even when the true distribution is a complex continuous function, what is the concept called?
Answer: B

Gibbs Sampling.

50. What is Multidimensional Scaling?
Answer: A

Technique used to find a two-dimensional representation of a dataset that visualizes the level of similarity of individual cases.

51. What is a Genetic Algorithm?
Answer: D

Chooses the strongest solution among a pool of random solutions, which is the one with the lowest cost, through modification and trait combination techniques.

52. What is the algorithm used by recommender systems to automatically predict the preferences of a smaller set of users by collecting those of many users, called?
Answer: B

Collaborative Filtering.

53. Which of the following best describes Stacking?
Answer: D

Method of training an algorithm to combine the predictions of multiple models or algorithms as additional inputs to the already available data.

54. You are looking at ways of implementation in deep learning in Weka. Which of the following can be considered as a relevant way?
Answer: D

Exploiting deep learning implementations for R with the use of MLRClassifier from the RPlugin package.

55. What is an open-source software library for JVM and Java, that supports a wide range of deep learning algorithms, called?
Answer: A

Deeplearning4j.

56. What is Unsupervised Learning?
Answer: B

Applications don't receive any training with examples, but learn by finding structure within a given set of data to recognize groups that exist within them.

57. You want to know more about the weakness of Bayesian classifier. Which of the following can be considered as a weakness?
Answer: C

Classifier cannot learn about combinations as features are given probabilities individually.

58. What is the type of regularization used while training a learner with an iterative method, in order to prevent overfitting, called?
Answer: D

Early Stopping.

59. You are looking at neural networks that have an internal state, as the connections between their units form a directed cycle. What are they called?
Answer: D

Recurrent Neural Networks.

60. What is a Support Vector Machine?
Answer: B

A supervised learning model, where a few support vectors or critical boundary instances are chosen from each class, to build a linear discriminant function.

61. What is Hierarchical Clustering?
Answer: A

A cluster analysis technique that builds a hierarchy of groups by constantly merging the two groups that are most similar.

62. You are looking at a field concerned with the interactions between computers and human languages and programming computers to manipulate large sets of languages. What is the field called?
Answer: D

NLP.

63. What is an EM Algorithm?
Answer: D

An iterative method to determine MLE or MAP for models that depend on unobserved latent variable, which uses two steps, the E Step and the M Step, to do so.

64. Which of the following best describes Additive Logistic Regression?
Answer: C

Algorithm for class probability estimation, which can get an algorithm for classification by using additive regression alongside logit transformation.

65. Which iterative optimization algorithm goes with the negative of the gradient, to find the local minimum of a function?
Answer: B

Gradient Descent.

66. You are looking at a boosting algorithm that maximizes probability when base learner minimizes squared error, which can be used in multi-class problems. What is the algorithm called?
Answer: D

LogitBoost.

67. What is a statistical Markov model where the system in context is assumed to be a Markov process with hidden or unobserved states, called?
Answer: C

Hidden Markov Model.

68. You are looking at an open-source deep learning toolkit developed by Microsoft Research, which describes neural networks as a series of computational steps. What is the toolkit called?
Answer: C

CNTK.

69. Which of the following can be considered as a relevant way of implementing deep learning in Weka?
Answer: A

Using the wrapper classifiers available in the third-party DeepLearning4J package.

70. You are looking at a concept that is used for inference in graphical models with cyclic structures, or for implementing Bayesian methods. What is the concept called?
Answer: B

Sampling.

71. What is Long Short Term Memory?
Answer: D

An RNN that uses a combination of hidden units and remembers values over arbitrary intervals, which tackles the vanishing gradient problem.

72. What is the technique in NLP that analyzes relationships between a set of documents and their terms, by creating a set of concepts related to the documents and terms, called?
Answer: A

Latent Semantic Analysis.

73. Which of the following best describes the capabilities of Neural Networks?
Answer: D

Capable of learning to do new tasks, and progressively improving performance, by looking at examples, and without being specifically programmed.

74. What is the method called that, if base learner reduces squared error, can minimize squared error for the ensemble, and perform automatic attribute selection, and

prevent overfitting?
Answer: A

Additive Regression.

75. Which of the following best describes Decision Trees?
Answer: C

Predictive machine learning method that adopts a transparent way of classifying observations, and sequencing what look like a set of if-then statements, into a tree.

76. You want to know more about the ways of implementation in deep learning in Weka. Which of the following can be considered as a relevant way?
Answer: A

Accessing Python-based deep learning libraries through the PyScript package.

77. What is a Factor Graph?
Answer: D

A probabilistic graphical model with two types of nodes, variable nodes and factor nodes, for each function, with edges connecting factor nodes to their variables.

78. What is Restricted Boltzmann Machine (RBM)?
Answer: A

A stochastic neural network that learns a probability distribution over a set of inputs, only with the restriction that its neurons should form a bipartite graph.

79. What is the method of using optimization algorithms to select values that minimize the output of a cost function, called?
Answer: B

Optimization.

80. What is a type of neural network called, where the hidden units are not random variables, hence the connections between the units do not form a cycle?
Answer: B

Deep Feedforward Networks.

81. What is the statistical model of representing probability distributions in a graphical way, drawn out as a network of nodes connected by directed edges, as an acyclic graph, called?
Answer: A

Bayesian Networks.

82. Which of the following can be best described as Recommender Systems?
Answer: B

Subclass of a filtering system that aims at predicting a user's preference to a given item.

83. What is a Markov Chain?
Answer: D

A Markov process that has either discrete index set, or discrete state space, usually representing time.

84. Which of the following best describes Test Set?
Answer: A

Set of data used to evaluate the strength and usability of a predictive relationship.

85. You are looking at a machine learning method based on learning data representation, instead of the traditional task-specific algorithms. What is the method called?
Answer: B

Deep Learning.

86. You are looking at an open-source script language based on the Lua programming language, that offers several algorithms for deep learning. What is the concept called?

Answer: C

Torch.

17

Answers To Bioinformatics

1. What is the method that uses background correction, normalization, and summarization to preprocess probe intensities and make biologically relevant conclusions possible, called?
   Answer: D
   Micro-Array Preprocessing.

2. When GO numbers are found by using the get function to extract a list from annotation files, and to select them with evidence, the subset function is used. What is the concept called?
   Answer: A
   Searching GO Numbers and Evidence.

3. What is the process of testing if genes with significant p-values in a t-test, occur more often within a certain chromosome, called?
   Answer: D
   Significance per Chromosome.

4. Which of the following can be considered as a Step for Gene Filtering by a Biological Term?
   Answer: B
   Define a function to collect appropriate GO numbers.

5. You want to find out ways of Applying Linear Models to Micro-Array Data. Which of the following is the most relevant way?
   Answer: C
   By using ANOVA.

6. What is Searching an Annotation Package?
   Answer: C
   The get function can be used to search for a name in an environment once the content of the environment is converted into a list and part of it printed on the screen.

7. Which of the following can be considered as a way to Obtain GO Parents and Children Identifiers?
   Answer: B
   Vector: If you have a list of GO identifiers, you can collect the ontology, parents, and children identifiers in a vector.

8. You are looking at Ways to Obtain GO Parents and Children Identifiers. Which of the following can be considered as a relevant way?
   Answer: B

Probe Selection: Start with probe number, find GO identifiers, obtain its parents, and transform them into probes.

9. What is Probe Data?
   Answer: A

   Raw data obtained by measuring the intensity of hybridization of probe to the target molecule.

10. You want to know more about Steps for Gene Filtering by a Biological Term. Which of the following can be considered as a relevant step?
    Answer: C

    Combine the term to be used with the previous filter.

11. Which of the following is a relevant Gene Filtering Method?
    Answer: D

    By combining many filters.

18

Answers To Python and Libraries

1. Which open-source library of machine learning algorithms is written in Java, for data mining tasks like classification, regression, etc.?
   Answer: B

   Weka.

2. Which of the following best describes Matplotlib?
   Answer: D

   A 2D plotting library for Python and NumPy, that offers an object-oriented API for embedding plots into applications.

3. What is Python?
   Answer: C

   An object-oriented, interpreted, high-level programming language that offers code readability, and constructs for writing large and small scale programs clearly.

4. The occurrence when two different keys are hashed to the same slot, or have the same hash code, is called as:
   Answer: B

   Hash Table Collision.

5. What is TensorFlow?
   Answer: B

   Library for machine learning, that uses data flow graphs to create and train neural networks to identify and analyze patterns analogous to human learning and reasoning.

6. What is an open-source topic modeling and vector space modeling toolkit for Python, designed to deal with large text collections, called?
   Answer: B

   Gensim.

7. Which of the following best describes PyBrain?
   Answer: C

   A neural networks library for Python that provides flexible yet high-performance algorithms for machine learning tasks, and environments to test and compare them.

8. Which of the following best describes Python MySQL?
   Answer: C

Enables Python programs to access MySQL databases, using an API that is compliant with the Python Database API Specification v2.0 (PEP 249).

9. You are looking at a problem where, a set of items with a value and a weight are chosen to fit a maximum weight limit, while keeping the total value high. What is the problem called?
Answer: B

Knapsack Problem.

10. A platform helps build Python programs for statistical and symbolic natural language processing for English written in Python. What is the platform called?
Answer: A

NLTK.

11. What is Theano?
Answer: D

Open-source numerical computation library for Python that enables efficient defining and optimizing of mathematical expressions that involve multi-dimensional arrays.

CPSIA information can be obtained
at www.ICGtesting.com
Printed in the USA
LVHW03s0204180918
590504LV00001B/60/P